A DAY IN
SEOUL

A DAY IN SEOUL

A Korean cookbook

Julian Kim

Smith Street Books

모두투어
한국일보
서중물류

INTRODUCTION

Seoul is a city where tradition and modernity live side by side. You only need to stand in Gwanghwamun Square in the centre of the city and you'll witness this contrast in full: the majestic Gyeongbokgung Palace, a symbol of pride in the Joseon dynasty (Korea's last and longest-running imperial dynasty), sits perfectly framed by the soaring glass towers of the 21st century. This is the spirit of Seoul – where the past and future dine at the same table.

Seoul is divided by the Han River, but the essence of the city is emotionally and culturally connected across this divide. To the north lies Gangbuk, the historic Old Town, which is home to royal palaces, traditional markets and tranquil tea houses. Here, the soul of the city simmers gently over a low flame.

In Seoul's south, the neighbourhood of Gangnam represents innovation – this is the home of the city's skyscrapers, luxury fashion and K-Beauty brands and avant-garde architecture – a sizzling hub of creativity and transformation. Yet even here, tucked between the glamorous stores, you'll find noodle shops hand-pulling kalguksu and stalls selling savoury jeon (pancakes).

The city's culinary roots – drawn from royal court cuisine and aristocratic homes – have evolved into a refined yet accessible food culture which has captivated the world. In just one day you can savour temple cuisine in Bukchon, sip specialty coffee in Seongsu and finish the night with spicy dakbal (chicken feet) at a pojangmacha (street stall) in Jongno. In Seoul, you're never forced to choose between old and new. You're invited to enjoy both.

Though it was once considered a hidden gem of East Asia, in recent years Seoul has been recognised as a captivating metropolis. Today's visitors are drawn in by Korea's most powerful export – its culture. From the electrifying beats of K-Pop to the gripping narratives of K-Dramas and K-Films, the global embrace of Korean culture has sparked a curiosity around the world for all things Korean. At the centre of this fascination is Korean cuisine, which has captivated the world's taste buds. From Michelin-starred bibimbap to humble street-side tteokbokki, Korean cuisine has quietly but powerfully entered the global culinary mainstream. K-Food is no longer a niche – it's a movement that is reshaping the way the world eats. And arguably nowhere offers a more vibrant entry point to the diversity of Korean food than its capital city.

Today Seoul stands proudly among the world's top gastronomic destinations – rivalling Tokyo, Bangkok and even Paris in its diversity, creativity and accessibility. From a vegan temple food cafe in the Old Town neighbourhood of Insadong to a sleek bar serving modern Korean food in the trendy Itaewon district, the city continues to reinterpret its culinary traditions for the world without losing its character.

In 2024 I founded Seoul Cooking Club so that visitors to the city could experience an authentic cultural experience. Since then, we have welcomed thousands of guests into our classes who are eager to immerse themselves in Korean culture. We've seen how the smallest gestures – rolling kimbap (seaweed rolls), stirring jjigae (stew), discovering the stories behind everyday banchan (side dishes) – become bridges to understanding. Cooking opens hearts.

A Day in Seoul is a heartfelt journey through the alleyways, markets and stories that simmer in every kitchen of this city. This book will invite you to start your day with a quiet bowl of juk (rice porridge) in a hanok courtyard and end it with sizzling samgyeopsal (Korean BBQ pork belly) under neon lights. It is a window into the lives of the people who live, breathe and cook in this extraordinary city.

This book features more than 80 carefully selected recipes, arranged around the rhythm of a typical Korean day – from breakfast to late-night snacks. The recipes in this book have been written by the chefs I work with, and each dish is accompanied by cultural context – when it's eaten, where and why.

Alongside these dishes, you'll find travel recommendations and cooking tips which will introduce you to the key dishes and the values that underpin Korean cuisine. You don't need to speak Korean to learn about our food, you only need the courage to take one bite at a time.

Whether you're planning your first visit to Seoul, are reminiscing on past travels, or cooking from the other side of the world, I hope this book will bring you closer to the heartbeat of Korea – one recipe, one story, one shared meal at a time. We've poured our passion and expertise into these pages. Now it's your turn to taste the true spirit of Korea, dish by dish.

The table is set. Seoul is calling. Let's begin.

CHEF'S NOTES

Welcome to the vibrant world of Korean cuisine! In Seoul, food is more than just sustenance – it's a reflection of Korea's history, seasons, and our deep appreciation for balance. We hope this book helps you explore and enjoy the unique flavours that make Korean food so special!

Korean cuisine uses a variety of grains, fresh vegetables, seafood and meat, all transformed into an incredible array of dishes, from hearty stews to delicate seasoned vegetable side dishes.

This diversity also extends to a fascinating range of fermented foods such as kimchi, a staple you'll find on almost every table, and various savoury jang (pastes). These condiments and fermented foods preserve fresh seasonal ingredients, and add incredible depth of flavour to all kinds of dishes. Many of the recipes in this book call for Korean ingredients which are readily available from Korean or Asian grocery stores. You can read more about these ingredients in the glossary on page 200.

A key aspect of Korean dining is the concept of a balanced meal. You can read more about the Korean bapsang (meal table setting) on page 34. Rice (bap) is a staple of the Korean diet (see page 184) and is served with most meals (especially soups and stews), alongside numerous banchan (side dishes).

This book uses 15 ml (½ fl oz) tablespoons.

Elly, Olivia, Grace, Sally
Seoul Cooking Club Chef Team

A NOTE FOR TRAVELLERS

From iconic sights to hidden gems, it's easy to understand why over 17 million tourists visited South Korea in 2024, exploring everything from Busan to Jeju Island, Jeonju to the East Sea and, of course, Seoul, the country's capital.

Whether you're here for one day or one month, Seoul will surprise, delight and inspire you. Welcome to a city where every corner tells a story. Here is some guidance on basic etiquette to make your trip to Seoul a breeze.

General etiquette

- In traditional spaces such as hanok (traditional Korean houses), temples, tea houses or traditional restaurants with floor seating, you may be required to remove your shoes before entering.
- When visiting temples, maintain silence and behave respectfully. Do not shout, run or touch sacred objects. Bowing slightly to monks is appreciated as a sign of courtesy.
- Some temples or historic sites prohibit photography. Always look for signs and ask if you are unsure.
- Koreans value quiet and orderly public behaviour. Keep your voice down, especially when taking phone calls or standing in queues.
- Korea has a strict recycling system. Be sure to separate food waste, plastics and general trash accordingly.
- Korean society is deeply rooted in Confucian values. Age and social hierarchy influence language and behaviour. Even as a visitor, showing basic respect and politeness, especially to the older generation, is important.

Basic dining etiquette

- When dining out at a restaurant, it is customary to greet staff when entering. Saying 'Annyeonghaseyo' (Hello) when entering a restaurant or cafe creates a positive impression.
- It is polite to wait for a staff member to show you to a table instead of seating yourself at a restaurant.
- Korean meals often come with side dishes known as banchan. It is customary to use clean chopsticks or spoons to serve yourself from shared plates.
- Avoid sticking chopsticks or spoons upright in your rice bowl – this is considered bad luck as it resembles a traditional ritual of offering food for the dead.
- Slurping or eating loudly is generally discouraged and considered rude in Korea.
- Meals are typically shared, reflecting the Korean values of jeong (affection) and community. A phrase like 'Gachi bap meok-eo-yo' (Let's have a meal together) carries a deep meaning of connection and goodwill.

Helpful Korean phrases for visitors

- 'Annyeonghaseyo' (Hello)
- 'Gamsahamnida' (Thank you)
- 'Jal meogeosseumnida' (Thank you for the meal)
- 'Shil lae hammida ' (Excuse me)

전자타운
올바른생활카드
NH농협카드

The Coffee Bean & Tea Leaf

더현대서울

EARLY

CU

FUROA

Forget the usual toast and cereal for breakfast. In Seoul, the morning meal is typically a light and savoury affair of rice, soup or porridge, offering a balanced start to the day.

As with all meals in Korea, rice is central to the morning meal, and is often accompanied by comforting soups and simple side dishes which nourish the body (and sometimes even help it to recover from whatever happened the night before!).

For me, the real magic of a Korean breakfast lies in its ability to be both simple and deeply comforting – and you can't get more simple than Nurungji (scorched rice, page 20). It's a beloved dish made from the crispy, toasted layer of rice from the bottom of a pot. It can be served as is, or you can pour over some hot water and cook it down to create a subtly flavoured porridge soup called nurungji-tang that's as perfect to eat in the morning as it is easy on the stomach. Yachae juk (vegetable porridge, page 21) is another gentle option, perfect for a light and comforting start, especially on cooler mornings.

If you're after something more substantial, my favourite way to start the day is with a bowl of Sogogi mu guk (beef radish soup, page 33) – the clear, warm broth gently soothes the stomach while the beef adds a satisfying heartiness.

For those who have indulged a bit too much the night before, a big bowl of Hwangtae haejangguk (dried pollock hangover soup, page 35) is a true lifesaver. This savoury soup is made with dried pollock fish, tofu and bean sprouts and is a famous Korean hangover cure.

While a sit-down breakfast is favourable, modern Seoul is a city that never stops. For busy commuters, quick and delicious on-the-go options are essential. One of my favourites for its convenience and balanced nutrition is Gimbap (page 29), which are portable rolls packed with seasoned rice, various vegetables, egg, and sometimes meat, all wrapped tightly in seaweed. Another favourite is Gilgeori toast (Korean street toast, page 25). A uniquely Korean take on a sandwich, this popular street food features thick toasted bread, a sweet-and-savoury omelette with finely chopped vegetables, often finished with a drizzle of ketchup and a sprinkle of sugar. It's a surprisingly addictive and satisfying quick bite that feels like a real treat on busy mornings!

JEONG CULTURE

A story of food and community.

In Korea, food is far more than just sustenance; it's a powerful language of love, care and connection. This deep-seated bond is embodied in the unique Korean concept of 'jeong'. While difficult to translate directly, jeong encompasses feelings of affection, attachment, empathy and a profound sense of human connection that develops through shared experiences. And often, these experiences revolve around food.

Eating together in Korea goes beyond simply sharing a meal. It's an act that actively fosters bonds, strengthens relationships and builds a sense of community. When Koreans share food, they're not just offering a dish; they're extending a piece of their jeong. This might be seen in a grandmother insisting you eat more food, a friend sharing a particularly delicious side dish from their plate, or neighbours exchanging homemade treats. In Korea, the act of giving and receiving food creates lasting emotional ties.

The most common example of jeong in practice is kimjang, a grand, traditional annual event where families and communities come together to prepare enormous quantities of kimchi for the upcoming winter. (In fact, kimjang is so culturally significant that it's recognised by UNESCO as an Intangible Cultural Heritage of Humanity!) This usually happens in late November to early December, after the fall harvest, when cabbages are at their crispest and sweetest.

Kimjang is a huge undertaking, involving meticulously hand-coating brined cabbages with a vibrant red chilli paste mixture. It's a deeply communal process: people gather, sharing tasks, stories and laughter, often passing down family kimchi recipes through generations.

The kimchi made during kimjang isn't just for your own family; it's traditionally shared with neighbours and relatives, embodying jeong principles by strengthening community ties and ensuring everyone has enough of this essential staple through the cold months.

Even in a bustling city like Seoul, the spirit of jeong remains a powerful force. While grand traditions like kimjang still exist in the city – often taking place in the communal spaces of apartment complexes – jeong is most often found in the small, everyday acts of sharing food. It's a neighbour sharing a fresh batch of kimchi or banchan, a friend dropping off a warm bowl of soup. These simple gestures prove that food is a powerful way to build connection and community in a modern metropolis.

NURUNGJI / NURUNG-JI-TANG

SCORCHED RICE / SCORCHED RICE SOUP

Nurungji is the name for the delicious scorched rice from the bottom of the pot. It is a beloved Korean delicacy with a fascinating history. Born of frugality, the toasted rice was traditionally rehydrated into a soothing porridge known as nurungji-tang, often enjoyed for its digestive benefits and comforting warmth. Today, these crispy, nutty morsels are enjoyed as a healthy snack or a soothing soup, showcasing Korea's ingenious culinary heritage of turning something humble into a delightful treat.

With its subtle toasted flavour and warm, soft consistency, nurungji-tang makes a gentle, comforting and easily digestible breakfast – a perfect way to start the day.

SERVES 2

370 g (2 cups) leftover cooked white rice (Bap, page 186); cold rice works best

1 Pour 125 ml (½ cup) water into a non-stick frying pan. Using a spatula or your hands, spread the cold cooked rice as thinly and evenly as possible across the bottom of the pan.

2 Place the pan over medium heat. The key to good nurungji is to toast the rice slowly and patiently, without stirring, until it forms a crisp, golden-brown crust underneath; this can take 15–25 minutes.

3 Using a spatula, carefully flip the rice crust over and toast the other side for about 10 minutes, until it also becomes golden brown and firm.

4 Remove the nurungji from the pan and leave to cool completely, until dry and crispy. Enjoy as is, or turn into scorched rice soup (nurungji-tang; see below). Store in an airtight container or zip-lock bag in a cool dark place for up to a week, or in the freezer for several months.

5 To make nurungji-tang, transfer the crispy nurungji to a small saucepan. Add 500 ml (2 cups) water and bring to the boil. Reduce the heat and simmer, stirring occasionally, for about 10 minutes, until the rice softens and breaks apart, forming a comforting porridge. Serve warm, with your favourite side dishes.

YACHAE JUK

VEGETABLE PORRIDGE

Symbolising health and comfort, this versatile porridge is a beloved staple in Korean daily life. While primarily a gentle meal for when you're feeling unwell, especially with an upset stomach as it is easily digestible and contains vital nutrients, it's also a popular light breakfast, providing a warm, comforting start to the day.

SERVES 2

- 1 tablespoon sesame oil
- ⅓ carrot, finely diced
- ½ zucchini (courgette), finely diced
- ¼ white onion, finely diced
- 40 g (1½ oz) fresh shiitake mushrooms
- 220 g (1 cup) short-grain white rice, washed and drained
- 1 teaspoon toasted sesame seeds
- gim-garu (shredded roasted seaweed flakes), to garnish (optional)

1 Place a saucepan over low heat and drizzle in the sesame oil. Add all the diced carrot, zucchini, onion and mushrooms and saute for about 5 minutes, stirring occasionally, until they become slightly translucent and softened.

2 Add the washed rice and saute together with the vegetables for 2–3 minutes, stirring constantly, ensuring the rice is lightly coated with oil.

3 Pour in 1 litre (4 cups) water. Increase the heat to medium-high and bring the mixture to a rolling boil, stirring occasionally to prevent sticking.

4 Once boiling, reduce the heat to medium-low. Continue to simmer for about 10 minutes, stirring frequently to prevent the rice sticking to the bottom of the pan. The rice should begin to break down and the porridge will start to thicken.

5 Continue to simmer until the rice is fully cooked and soft, and the porridge has reached your desired thickness and consistency; this may take an additional 5–10 minutes, depending on your preferred texture.

6 Ladle the hot porridge into bowls. Garnish with the toasted sesame seeds and gim-garu, if desired, and serve immediately.

LABELESS
LABELESS
LABELESS
칠성
CHILSUNG CIDER
함덕수퍼
Coca-Cola
Chilsung Cider
pepsi
에스원
SECOM
아빠의청춘
국순당
TERRA

GILGEORI TOAST

KOREAN STREET TOAST

Though its exact origins are debated, this unique sweet and savoury sandwich, often packed with egg, cabbage and sugar, is now a ubiquitous sight on the streets of Seoul, and an iconic street food breakfast to fuel busy mornings. It's the ultimate grab-and-go meal that perfectly captures the dynamic energy of the city.

MAKES 2

- 4 large eggs
- pinch of fine sea salt
- 100 g (1⅓ cups) finely shredded wombok (Chinese cabbage)
- ⅓ carrot, finely julienned
- ¼ white onion, finely julienned
- 30 g (1 oz) margarine
- 4 slices white sandwich bread
- vegetable oil, for pan-frying
- 2 tablespoons white sugar
- tomato ketchup, for drizzling

1 Crack the eggs into a bowl, add the salt and whisk well until combined. Add the cabbage, carrot and onion and stir to combine thoroughly.

2 Heat a frying pan over medium heat. Add half of the margarine. Once melted, place two of the bread slices in the pan and toast on both sides for a minute or two until golden brown and crispy. Remove to a cutting board, then repeat with the remaining margarine and bread slices.

3 Clean the pan and add a drizzle of vegetable oil. Pour half the egg mixture into the pan, shaping it into a rectangle that matches the size of your bread slices. Cook over medium heat for 4–6 minutes, until the bottom is golden brown and the egg is mostly set. Carefully flip, then cook the other side until fully cooked through. Remove from the pan, then repeat with the remaining egg mixture, to make two egg patties.

4 To assemble the toasts, top two of the toasted bread slices with an egg patty. Evenly sprinkle about 1 tablespoon sugar over each egg patty. Drizzle a little ketchup over the sugar, then top with the other toasted bread slices.

5 Carefully cut the assembled toasts in half diagonally. Enjoy immediately, while still warm.

GYERAN-MARI

ROLLED OMELETTE

Gyeran-mari is a great breakfast side dish because it's quick and easy to prepare, offers a good source of protein to help you start your day with energy, and its mild, savoury flavour is also gentle on the stomach early in the morning. For generations, gyeran-mari has also been a popular lunchbox staple, lovingly prepared by mothers. It's a comforting treat that embodies the warmth of everyday Korean home cooking and childhood memories.

MAKES 1 ROLL; SERVES 2

- 5 large eggs
- 1 tablespoon finely diced onion
- 1 tablespoon finely chopped spring onion (scallion)
- 1 tablespoon finely diced carrot
- 2 teaspoons finely diced red chilli or bell pepper (capsicum)
- ½ teaspoon mirim (Korean rice cooking wine)
- ½ teaspoon fine sea salt
- pinch of ground black pepper
- 2 tablespoons vegetable oil
- tomato ketchup, to serve

1 Crack the eggs into a bowl and whisk thoroughly using a balloon whisk. Strain the egg mixture through a fine-mesh sieve for a smoother texture.

2 Add the finely chopped vegetables, mirim, salt and pepper and whisk thoroughly until all the ingredients are well combined.

3 Heat the vegetable oil in a non-stick frying pan over medium heat. Once the pan is preheated, reduce the heat to low. Pour about two-thirds of the egg mixture evenly into the pan, forming a thin layer that covers the bottom.

4 As the egg mixture begins to set underneath, but while the top is still slightly moist, use a rubber or silicone spatula to gently roll the omelette from one end to the other, rolling tightly to prevent it from tearing.

5 Once fully rolled, slide the omelette to one end of the pan. Keeping the heat on low, pour the remaining egg mixture into the empty space in the pan, allowing it to slightly connect with the rolled omelette. Continue to roll the omelette, incorporating the new egg layer, until it is fully rolled.

6 Transfer the finished omelette to a cutting board. Let it cool for 2–3 minutes, as slicing it while it is too hot can cause the fillings to spill, resulting in a less clean cut.

7 Once cooled slightly, slice the omelette into bite-sized pieces, holding the knife at a slight angle for a wider, more visually appealing cross-section.

8 Serve with ketchup on the side as a breakfast side dish; the gyeran-mari will also keep well in an airtight container in the fridge for 3–4 days.

Note
Finely dicing the vegetables ensures they mix well with the beaten egg, resulting in a neat omelette shape.

GIMBAP

RICE ROLLED WITH VEGETABLES

Gimbap, Korea's iconic seaweed-rolled rice dish, is Seoul's ultimate on-the-go meal, and an everyday delight. It's a cherished comfort food – whether as a quick breakfast for busy office workers or a nostalgic picnic treat lovingly prepared by mothers for children's school trips.

The recipe below is the classic version of gimbap. Unlike Japanese sushi, which is made with vinegared rice, gimbap is typically filled with fresh seafood and served chilled, Korean gimbap is made with rice seasoned with sesame oil and salt, is filled with cooked ingredients and is often enjoyed at room temperature.

Today, gimbap continues to evolve with countless modern variations, embracing diverse and creative fillings. It truly remains a versatile staple that is deeply woven into the fabric of Korean daily life.

MAKES 4 ROLLS

600 g (3¼ cups) warm cooked short-grain white rice (Bap, page 186)

2 tablespoons sesame oil (for the rice), plus extra for brushing over the rolls

1 teaspoon fine sea salt

1 tablespoon toasted sesame seeds

4 sheets toasted gimbap gim (dried seaweed) or toasted nori

1 Place the warm cooked rice in a large bowl with the sesame oil, sea salt and toasted sesame seeds. Mix gently with a rice paddle or spatula until everything is well combined and the rice is seasoned evenly. Set aside while preparing the fillings.

2 Place the cucumber in a small bowl, lightly sprinkle with salt and leave to sit for 10 minutes to draw out the excess water.

3 Meanwhile, lightly saute the carrot strips in a frying pan over medium heat with a tiny bit of vegetable oil for 1–2 minutes, until slightly tender but still crunchy. Season with a pinch of salt, remove from the pan and leave to cool.

4 Beat the eggs lightly with a pinch of salt. Wipe the pan clean, lightly oil and place over medium-low heat. Pour in the whisked eggs and cook for 2–3 minutes, until golden underneath and about 80 per cent set on top. Carefully flip and cook for another 1–2 minutes, until the other side is also golden brown. Slide the omelette onto a cutting board and slice into long, thin strips about 20 cm (8 in) long.

5 Drain the cucumber batons and pat dry with paper towel. Ensure the burdock strips, danmuji and crab sticks are also patted dry and ready to use.

6 Place one sheet of seaweed on a bamboo rolling mat, with the rough side facing up.

Continues next page →

Fillings

- ½ short cucumber, seeds removed, cut into 20 cm (8 in) batons
- fine sea salt
- 100 g (3½ oz) carrot, peeled and cut into matchsticks 2–3 mm (¹⁄₁₆ in) thick
- vegetable oil, for pan-frying
- 4 eggs
- 60 g (2 oz) store-bought braised burdock strips for gimbap (soy-sauce seasoned) (see Note)
- 4 long strips store-bought danmuji (pickled yellow radish) (see Note)
- 4 imitation crab sticks
- 4 strips ham, 20 cm (8 in) long and 1 cm (½ in) thick

7 Spread about one-quarter of the seasoned rice evenly over the sheet, leaving a 2.5 cm (1 in) gap at the top edge. Don't press the rice down too hard, just spread it gently. Arrange a line of each filling ingredient neatly across the rice, 2.5 cm (1 in) from the bottom line of the sheet.

8 Carefully lift the bottom edge of the bamboo mat and roll the seaweed sheet and fillings tightly upwards to meet the top edge. Press down firmly as you roll to ensure the roll is tight.

9 Lightly rub the finished roll with a thin layer of sesame oil for extra shine and flavour.

10 Using a sharp, lightly oiled knife, carefully slice each roll into neat pieces 1.5–2 cm (½–¾ in) thick.

11 Arrange on a platter and serve immediately. Enjoy your homemade gimbap!

Note

The burdock strips and danmuji (pickled yellow radish) are key fillings for this gimbap, but you can improvise by using other pickled vegetables instead of danmuji, and substitute the burdock strips with sliced shiitake mushrooms sauteed with soy sauce and sugar.

우리은행
WOORI BANK
88 반포대교 Banpodaegyo(Br)
남산3호터널 Namsan 3(sam) Tunnel
60 을지로1가
Euljiro 1(il)-ga
31
숭례문
崇禮門
Sungnyemun
100m
1호터널
15분 예상

SOGOGI MU GUK

BEEF AND RADISH SOUP

This clear, savoury beef and radish soup is Seoul's ultimate comfort in a bowl. In Korean cuisine, radish (mu) is a foundational vegetable, prized for its refreshing taste, digestive benefits and warming properties. Historically, beef (sogogi) was a precious ingredient reserved for special occasions and feasts; combining it with radish in a soup created a richer, more flavourful dish. This beloved preparation gradually spread beyond special events, becoming a cherished homemade staple throughout Korea.

Beef radish soup is ideal for breakfast because it offers a comforting yet nutritious start to the day. The mild broth, combined with the digestive enzymes from the radish, is gentle on an empty stomach, while the beef provides essential protein for sustained energy.

SERVES 4

250 g (9 oz) beef brisket
350 g (12½ oz) Korean radish
2 tablespoons sesame oil
1.4 litres (47 fl oz) Anchovy-kelp broth (page 192) or water
1 teaspoon minced garlic
2 tablespoons tuna extract (chamchi-aek)
2 tablespoons guk ganjang (Korean soup soy sauce), or to taste
fine sea salt, to taste (optional)
1 large spring onion (scallion), sliced diagonally
pinch of finely ground black pepper

1 Lightly pat the beef with paper towel to remove any excess blood. Cut the beef into bite-sized pieces.

2 Peel the radish and cut into slices about 5 mm (¼ in) thick, then cut into rectangles.

3 In a large saucepan, heat the sesame oil over medium heat. Add the beef and saute for 3–5 minutes, until just lightly browned. Add the radish and continue to cook for about 2 minutes, stirring occasionally, until the beef and radish are well combined.

4 Pour in the anchovy broth or water. Cover the pan and bring to the boil. As the soup comes to the boil, use a ladle or spoon to skim off any brown foam or impurities that rise to the surface – this will ensure a clear broth.

5 Reduce the heat to medium-low. Add the garlic and tuna extract, then season with the guk ganjang to taste, and salt if needed.

6 Add the spring onion and a pinch of black pepper. Simmer for another 2–3 minutes, until the spring onion is tender.

7 Serve immediately with warm rice (see pages 186 or 188) on the side.

Note

This soup can be made the day before. When gently reheated, the flavours will be richer and more cohesive, creating a deeper and more satisfying taste than when it was first cooked.

SOGOGI MIYEOK GUK

BEEF SEAWEED SOUP

In Korea, this soup is much more than just a dish; it's a profound symbol of care and celebration – a bowl full of love. Traditionally, it's a must-have for new mothers recovering from childbirth, as it was believed to aid healing and provide essential nutrients. This same nourishing soup is also central to every Korean's birthday, eaten to honour one's mother for her sacrifices and to wish for good health in the year ahead. It's a heartwarming culinary tradition, deeply connecting generations and marking life's significant moments.

Beef seaweed soup is also great for breakfast because it's nutritious, gentle and easy to digest, which helps you feel comfortable and sated for a long time.

SERVES 6

- 30 g (1 oz) miyeok (dried brown seaweed)
- 200 g (7 oz) beef brisket
- 2 tablespoons sesame oil
- 1 tablespoon guk ganjang (Korean soup soy sauce)
- 1 tablespoon minced garlic
- 1.5 litres (6 cups) water or Anchovy-kelp broth (page 192)
- 2 tablespoons tuna extract (chamchi-aek)
- 2 teaspoons coarse sea salt

1 Place the miyeok in a bowl, pour in enough water to cover completely, then leave to soak for 10–15 minutes, until fully rehydrated and soft. Rinse thoroughly under cold running water, gently rubbing the seaweed clean. Drain well, then cut into 4 cm (1½ in) pieces. Squeeze out any excess water.

2 Lightly pat the beef with paper towel to remove any excess blood. Cut the beef into bite-sized pieces.

3 Heat a saucepan over medium–low heat. Add the sesame oil, guk ganjang and garlic. Add the beef and saute for 2–3 minutes, stirring occasionally, until the beef is about halfway cooked and no longer red. Be careful not to burn the garlic.

4 Add the seaweed pieces and saute for another 2–3 minutes, stirring gently, until the seaweed becomes soft and slightly translucent; this step helps to develop a deeper flavour.

5 Pour in the water or anchovy broth. Add the tuna extract and salt. Increase the heat to high and bring the soup to a rolling boil. Reduce the heat to medium–low, cover the pan and let it simmer gently for 20–30 minutes, to allow the beef to become tender and the flavours to meld.

6 Taste the soup, season with additional salt or guk ganjang if desired, and serve.

Note

This soup can be made the day before. When gently reheated, the flavours will be richer and more cohesive, creating a deeper and more satisfying taste than when it was first cooked.

HWANGTAE HAEJANGGUK

DRIED POLLOCK HANGOVER SOUP

Waking up after a fun night out in Seoul? Koreans often reach for this comforting dried pollock soup as the ultimate hangover cure.

Pollock is considered a 'magical' fish in Korea because its culinary purpose changes depending on how it is prepared, transforming from fresh 'saengtae' to frozen 'dongtae' or dried 'bugeo'. The most highly prized pollock preparation is the 'hwangtae' which is used in this restorative soup – this pollock has been slowly air-dried in freezing winds, concentrating its flavour and nutrients.

Beyond its versatility, pollock is known as a beloved hangover cure – especially in this soothing soup – as it is rich in methionine, an amino acid that helps the liver break down alcohol. Light yet rich in flavour, this soup's mild broth is gentle on a sensitive stomach, providing essential hydration and nutrients to quickly restore the body after a big night out.

SERVES 4

- 70 g dried pollock slices (hwangtaechae), cut into 4 cm (1½ in) lengths
- 1 tablespoon sesame oil
- 200 g (7 oz) white radish, peeled and sliced into batons about 4 mm (⅛ in) thick
- 1 tablespoon minced garlic
- 500 ml (2 cups) store-bought beef bone broth (sagol gomtang yuksu)
- 1 teaspoon coarse sea salt
- 200 g (7 oz) firm tofu, cut into bite-sized pieces
- 100 g (3½ oz) soybean sprouts, washed and drained
- ½ large spring onion (scallion), sliced diagonally
- 1 tablespoon guk ganjang (Korean soup soy sauce)
- ground black pepper, to taste

1 Place the dried pollock in a bowl and cover with cold water. Leave to soak for about 15 minutes, until the fish becomes soft, then immediately and thoroughly squeeze out the water.

2 In a large saucepan, heat the sesame oil over medium heat. Add the rehydrated pollock, radish and garlic and saute for 5–7 minutes, stirring now and then, until the pollock pieces are lightly dry again.

3 Pour in the bone broth and 1.5 litres (6 cups) water. Add the sea salt. Cover the pan and bring to the boil, then reduce the heat to medium-low and simmer for 30 minutes.

4 Add the tofu, soybean sprouts, spring onion and guk ganjang. Simmer for another 5 minutes, allowing the sprouts to cook and the flavours to deepen.

5 Taste the soup and season with more salt or guk ganjang as needed.

6 Stir in a pinch of black pepper just before serving. Ladle the hot soup into bowls and enjoy its deep, savoury flavour and refreshing qualities.

Note

This soup can be made the day before. When gently reheated, the flavours will be richer and more cohesive, creating a deeper and more satisfying taste than when it was first cooked.

TTEOKGUK

SLICED RICE CAKE SOUP

Tteokguk, a comforting rice cake soup, is the quintessential dish for Seollal (Korean Lunar New Year), a major holiday where families gather to celebrate a fresh start. Traditionally, eating a bowl of tteokguk on the morning of Seollal symbolises gaining a year in Korea's unique age-counting system – leading to playful jokes like, 'I've had ten bowls, so I'm older than you!' In many ways this warm, nourishing soup marks the turning of the year, bringing wishes for health and prosperity to all who enjoy it.

SERVES 2

1 egg
vegetable oil, for pan-frying
150 g (5½ oz) beef brisket
2 tablespoons sesame oil, plus extra to serve
2 teaspoons minced garlic
2 tablespoons guk ganjang (Korean soup soy sauce)
350 g (12½ oz) sliced rice cakes (see Notes)
½ large spring onion (scallion), thinly sliced diagonally
1 teaspoon salt, or to taste
Gim gui (toasted seaweed, page 178), to garnish
ground black pepper, for sprinkling

Notes

The rice cakes used in this soup are called garaetteok – long, thick, cylindrical rice cakes made from non-glutinous rice flour, with a pure white colour and a firm, chewy texture. You will often find these rice cakes conveniently pre-sliced, ready to use for this soup, in the refrigerated section of Korean grocery stores, labelled as tteokguk-tteok.

If you want to slice your own garaetteok for this soup, slice the rice cylinders on the diagonal, about 5 mm (¼ in) thick. Cutting the slices on the diagonal creates wider, oval-shaped pieces that allow the rice cake to cook thoroughly, become tender and chewy, and absorb the flavour of the broth without falling apart.

This soup is best enjoyed straight away. If the rice cakes are left to sit in the broth for too long, they will become soggy and lose their signature chewy texture, and will also make the soup cloudy.

1 Crack the egg into a small bowl and lightly whisk. Strain the egg through a fine-mesh sieve for a smoother texture.

2 Heat a frying pan over medium heat and lightly grease with vegetable oil, then wipe off the excess oil with paper towel. Reduce the heat to low.

3 Pour a thin layer of the strained egg mixture into the pan, spreading it evenly. When the egg is mostly set but still slightly moist on top, gently slide a spatula underneath the centre and carefully flip it over, without tearing. Briefly cook the other side until set.

4 Transfer the egg to a cutting board. Once cooled, roll it up tightly and slice into thin strips. Set aside for garnishing.

5 Lightly pat the beef with paper towel to remove any excess blood. Cut into bite-sized pieces.

6 Place the beef in a saucepan with the sesame oil, 1 teaspoon of the garlic and 1 tablespoon of the guk ganjang. Saute over medium heat for 5–10 minutes, until the beef is lightly browned and fully cooked on the outside.

7 Pour in 900 ml (30½ fl oz) water and bring to a rolling boil over high heat. As the soup comes to the boil, use a ladle or spoon to skim off any foam or impurities that rise to the surface – this will ensure a clearer broth. Reduce the heat to medium, cover the pan and simmer for 10 minutes to allow the beef flavour to infuse into the broth.

8 Meanwhile, soak the rice cake slices in a bowl of water for 10 minutes to soften them.

9 Thoroughly drain the rice cake slices, then add them to the broth. Cook over medium heat for about 10 minutes, until the rice cakes are tender and float to the surface, indicating they are cooked.

10 Add the remaining guk ganjang, garlic and half the spring onion. Continue to cook until the soup boils once more, then taste and season with the salt as needed.

11 Ladle the hot soup into serving bowls. Garnish with the egg ribbons, gim gui and remaining spring onion. Sprinkle with black pepper and serve immediately, with an extra drizzle of sesame oil for extra flavour if desired.

BAPSANG & BANCHAN

Step into any Korean home or restaurant and you'll immediately notice the unique way a meal is served. Unlike Western dining where dishes arrive in courses, a Korean table, or bapsang, presents all the dishes at once.

You'll always find rice and soup on the table, but it's the colourful array of side dishes – the banchan – that truly defines the mood of the meal. The number of banchan that are included as part of a bapsang generally indicates how formal the meal is – as a rule, the more banchan on the table, the more formal the meal is.

A casual weekday breakfast would generally be a '3 cheop bapsang', which would typically include rice, soup and two banchan. Everyday family meals tend to be a '5 cheop bapsang', and include soup and four side dishes alongside the all-important rice.

More elaborate dinners or holiday parties follow a '7 cheop bapsang', with six banchan dishes served with the soup and rice. Grander settings with a higher cheop tier were historically reserved for royalty (kings could enjoy up to 11 different banchan dishes!). These more elaborate meals are a great opportunity to showcase the incredible variety Korean cuisine can offer.

Banchan serve to balance the five fundamental flavours – spicy, savoury, sour, sweet and bitter – creating a harmonious dining experience. Imagine a symphony of tastes and textures: spicy kimchi, savoury stir-fries, refreshing salads and earthy seasoned vegetables, all laid out to complement your rice and main dish. They are typically placed in the centre of the table and shared communally. One delightful surprise for many visitors to Korea is that banchan are refilled for free in restaurants, encouraging you to savour their incredible variety.

Banchan are always prepared using fresh, seasonal ingredients to ensure peak flavour and nutritional value. They aren't just appetisers; they are integral components to a meal that offer balance alongside vibrant and contrasting flavours, as well as essential nutrition. They are the true star of the Korean table.

Some beloved banchan that often grace the Korean table include:

- Samsaek namul (three-coloured seasoned vegetables, page 40)
- Myeolchi bokkeum (stir-fried small dried anchovies, page 182)
- Yachae jangajji (pickled vegetables, page 176)
- Gyeran-mari (rolled omelette, page 26)
- Oi muchim (cucumber salad, page 175)
- Baechu kimchi (Seoul-style kimchi, page 166)
- Kkakdugi (diced radish kimchi, page 172).

SAMSAEK NAMUL

THREE-COLOURED SEASONED VEGETABLES

In Korea, breakfast usually follows the same structure as lunch and dinner – rice and soup served alongside a variety of banchan (side dishes).

Being lighter, milder and easier to digest than other banchan, with less spice and salt, seasoned vegetable dishes known as namul are a common addition to breakfast as they are gentle on the stomach and not overpowering.

These three seasoned vegetable dishes – kong namul (bean sprouts), gosari namul (fern bracken) and sigeumchi namul (green spinach) – can be enjoyed individually as delicious side dishes, but when arranged beautifully on one plate as 'samsaek namul', they create a visually appealing harmony of colours and flavours.

These seasoned vegetables are also fantastic as key ingredients for Bibimbap (mixed rice with vegetables, page 62), when mixed together with warm rice and gochujang (Korean chilli paste).

SERVES 4 AS A SIDE DISH

Kong namul (bean sprouts)

- 300 g (10½ oz) soybean sprouts
- ⅓ teaspoon coarse sea salt
- 1 tablespoon sesame oil
- 1 tablespoon chopped spring onion (scallion), white part only
- 2 teaspoons minced garlic
- 2 teaspoons guk ganjang (Korean soup soy sauce)
- 1 teaspoon toasted sesame seeds

Kong namul

1 Gently rinse the soybean sprouts under cold running water, then drain thoroughly in a colander.

2 In a wide saucepan or wok, bring 250 ml (1 cup) water to a rolling boil over high heat. Once boiling, add the sea salt. Spread the soybean sprouts evenly in the pot and immediately put the lid on. Leave to steam for 3 minutes.

3 Open the lid, gently mix the sprouts from top to bottom, then quickly cover again and blanch for another 30 seconds.

4 Immediately transfer the blanched sprouts to a colander and rinse thoroughly under cold running water to stop the cooking process and maintain the crispness of the sprouts. Firmly squeeze out any excess water.

5 Place the drained sprouts in a bowl. Add all the remaining ingredients and gently toss together by hand, mixing well, until the sprouts are evenly coated.

6 Taste and season with more salt or guk ganjang if needed. You could also add some gochugaru (Korean chilli flakes) if you prefer it spicy. The sprouts are best enjoyed the same day for the freshest texture and flavour, but will keep in an airtight container in the fridge for 2–3 days.

Gosari namul (fern bracken)

- 100 g (3½ oz) dried gosari (fern bracken)
- 2 tablespoons perilla oil
- 1 tablespoon minced garlic
- 1 tablespoon guk ganjang (Korean soup soy sauce)
- 100 ml (3½ fl oz) Anchovy-kelp broth (page 192), or water
- 2 tablespoons chopped spring onion (scallion), white part only
- 1 teaspoon toasted sesame seeds
- fine sea salt, to taste (optional)

Gosari namul

1 Soak the dried gosari in lukewarm water for 6–8 hours or overnight, until fully rehydrated and soft, changing the water once or twice during soaking, if possible.

2 Remove and discard any tough stems or discoloured parts from the rehydrated gosari. Rinse thoroughly, place in a saucepan with enough water to fully submerge it, then bring to the boil. Cover the pan, reduce the heat to medium and gently simmer for 20–30 minutes.

3 Drain the gosari, then rinse several times under cold running water to remove any bitterness. Squeeze out the excess water, then cut into 5–7 cm (2–2¾ in) lengths.

4 Using the same saucepan, the perilla oil in the pan over medium heat. Add the garlic and saute until fragrant.

5 Add the guk ganjang and mix well, then stir-fry for 3–5 minutes.

6 Pour in the anchovy broth (or water), cover the pan and leave to simmer over medium-low heat for 5–7 minutes, to allow the gosari to absorb the flavours and become tender.

7 Once most of the liquid has evaporated, add the spring onion and stir-fry briefly for a final 3–5 minutes. Sprinkle with the toasted sesame seeds and mix them through.

8 Taste and season with salt if needed. The mixture will keep in an airtight container in the fridge for 3–5 days without a significant change in flavour or texture.

Continues next page →

Sigeumchi namul (green spinach)

- 300 g (10½ oz) spinach
- ⅓ teaspoon coarse sea salt
- 1 tablespoon sesame oil
- 1 tablespoon chopped spring onion (scallion), white part only
- 2 teaspoons minced garlic
- 2 teaspoons guk ganjang (Korean soup soy sauce)
- 1 teaspoon toasted sesame seeds

Sigeumchi namul

1 Trim and discard the root ends of the spinach and remove any yellowed or damaged leaves.

2 Bring a saucepan of water to a rolling boil. Once boiling, add the sea salt.

3 Add the spinach and blanch for 30 seconds to 1 minute, until the spinach is slightly tender but still has some crunch.

4 Immediately transfer the blanched spinach to a bowl of cold water to stop the cooking process and preserve its vibrant colour and crispness.

5 Drain the spinach well, then squeeze out the excess water using your hands, until the spinach is relatively dry.

6 Place the drained spinach in a bowl. Add all the remaining ingredients. Gently mix together by hand, tossing and lightly squeezing the spinach to ensure the seasonings are evenly distributed.

7 Taste and adjust the seasoning as needed. The spinach is best enjoyed the same day for the freshest texture and flavour, but will keep in an airtight container in the fridge for 2–3 days.

SOGOGI MECHURIAL JANGJORIM

BRAISED BEEF IN SOY SAUCE

A true staple in Korean homes, cherished by all ages, this comforting medley of tender braised beef with creamy quail eggs offers a savoury yet subtly sweet breakfast option.

Jangjorim is considered an ideal side dish for busy mornings due to its incredible convenience. Because it can be made well ahead of time, and is typically enjoyed cold, you can simply serve it straight from the fridge as a ready-to-eat accompaniment to a simple bowl of rice, saving you precious time. The flavours of the soy-based braising liquid deepen and meld with the beef and quail eggs as the dish cools, making it even more delicious when served cold.

It's the kind of reliable, protein-packed side dish that makes any Korean family meal feel complete and satisfying.

SERVES 4

- 400 g (14 oz) beef eye round, topside, silverside or round steak, cut into 3 cm (1¼ in) chunks
- 1 tablespoon white sugar
- 200 g (7 oz) quail eggs, boiled and peeled (see Note)

Broth

- 1.2 litres (41 fl oz) water
- 10 whole garlic cloves, peeled
- ½ white onion
- 1 spring onion (scallion), roughly chopped
- 2 sheets dasima (dried kelp)

Braising sauce

- 150 ml (5 fl oz) jin ganjang (Korean soy sauce)
- 90 ml mirim (Korean cooking rice wine)
- 3 tablespoons brown sugar
- 1 tablespoon oligo syrup
- 5 whole garlic cloves, peeled
- 1 small piece fresh ginger (approx. 1–2 cm/ ½–¾ in), peeled

Note
To hard-boil quail eggs, place them in a saucepan with plenty of cold water and bring to the boil. Reduce the heat and simmer for 3–4 minutes, then immediately transfer the eggs to an ice bath to cool. The eggs will be cooked perfectly and will now be easy to peel.

1 Place the beef in a bowl and cover with enough cold water to submerge it completely. Add the sugar to the water and let the beef soak for about 30 minutes to draw out impurities and tenderise the meat. Rinse the beef thoroughly under cold running water, then pat dry with paper towel to remove any excess blood.

2 While the beef is soaking, place all the broth ingredients in a large saucepan and bring to the boil over high heat. After boiling for 5 minutes, remove the dried kelp to prevent bitterness.

3 Add the drained beef to the boiling broth. Initially, leave to boil over high heat and, as impurities rise to the surface, carefully skim them off with a ladle or spoon to ensure a clean broth.

4 Reduce the heat to medium, then cover and simmer for about 40 minutes, or until the beef is tender. Remove the beef from the pan and leave to cool completely. Strain the broth through a fine-mesh sieve and set aside. Leave to cool, then skim off any excess fat from the surface of the broth.

5 Once the beef has cooled, use your hands to tear it into small, thin shreds along the grain.

6 Pour 600 ml (20½ fl oz) of the reserved broth into a clean saucepan. Add all the braising sauce ingredients. Add the shredded beef to the pan.

7 Bring the mixture to the boil, then reduce the heat to medium-low and simmer for 10 minutes, allowing the beef to absorb the flavours.

8 Add the peeled quail eggs and simmer for another 10 minutes, ensuring the eggs are well coated and heated through. Remove the ginger piece and garlic cloves.

9 Let the jangjorim cool completely, then transfer to an airtight container and refrigerate. Properly stored, it will keep in the fridge for up to 1 week. To prevent spoilage, always use a clean spoon to take out a portion.

MID

7344-116
A/S
애플서비스
4F
733-4165
ce1996
Forza 4F
하남 돼지집
맥주창고
CRAFT BEER
중고폰 매입판매
춘복참치
종각직영점 723-4558
숙박
₩50,000
대실
₩20,000
TOM N TOMS COFFEE
대실
₩20,000

In Seoul, lunch is a dynamic mealtime filled with a wide array of flavours and dining experiences.

While many cultures have distinct foods for breakfast, lunch and dinner, Korean cuisine often defies these strict boundaries. Many of the dishes you'll find in this chapter, from hearty stews and satisfying stir-fries to refreshing noodles, are versatile enough to be enjoyed at different times of the day. Whether you're a busy office worker grabbing a quick meal or a family gathering for a traditional feast, midday in Seoul offers a chance to recharge and savour a wide spectrum of flavours.

In the bustling rhythm of the city, the lunch hour for office workers is a crucial pause. It's a snapshot of Korean daily life, where traditional eating habits meet the city's fast pace. At the heart of this culture is baekban, a balanced and comforting set meal that offers a taste of home amidst the workday rush.

Baekban literally translates to 'white rice meal', but it is more than just rice; it's a foundation of rice and soup accompanied by an array of diverse banchan – small, flavourful side dishes. Baekban is a popular lunchtime choice because it offers a hearty, healthy and surprisingly affordable meal, often featuring fresh, seasonal ingredients that change daily. For busy professionals with limited lunch breaks (in Korea they are typically no longer than one hour), the quick service of baekban allows for efficient time management.

A baekban meal usually centres around a main dish, often a comforting stew or a savoury stir-fry. My favourite is Dakgalbi (spicy stir-fried chicken, page 55) which I normally get from my favourite spot in Hongdae. This hearty and spicy stir-fried chicken dish is usually cooked tableside with vegetables and rice cakes in a gochujang-based sauce. Another delicious option is Dwaejigogi kimchi jjigae baekban (pork kimchi stew, page 81), which is a quintessential Korean stew made from kimchi, pork and tofu – it's famously spicy and tangy thanks to the kimchi.

One of my go-to spots for a great-value jjigae baekban is Ttukbaegi-jip in Jongno. It's the kind of place that's hard to find in the city, where for less than $10 you get a hearty stew and plenty of savoury side dishes. The best part? The rice is served in a big bowl, perfect for mixing with the banchan to create your own quick bibimbap.

If I'm ever near Gyeongbokgung Station and craving a comforting meal, I head straight to Jeonju Kongnamul Gukbapjip for their incredible Sundubu jjigae (soft tofu stew, page 82) – I've honestly lost count of how many times I've been there.

And for those lunchtimes where time isn't a concern, I love going to Ogeunnae Dakgalbi in Yongsan with my colleagues. We all sit around a large iron pan to cook the spicy chicken together. The meal isn't complete until we've followed the unspoken rule of frying rice in the leftover sauce – it's a deeply satisfying and nostalgic tradition.

TTEOKBOKKI

STIR-FRIED RICE CAKES

Often hailed as the 'soul food' of Koreans, tteokbokki is an iconic, irresistibly addictive dish of chewy rice cakes swimming in a fiery, sweet and savoury gochujang sauce. Tteokbokki also lies at the heart of Korea's 'bunsik' street food culture – one of many quick, cheerful, absolutely delicious and incredibly affordable bites sold by bustling shops on virtually every block near schools and office buildings, catering to those looking for a satisfying snack or a quick, hearty lunch. Bunsik dishes like this are an essential part of the modern Korean food landscape, perfectly fitting the pace of Seoul life.

SERVES 4

- 4 rectangular eomuk sheets (processed seafood sheets; see Notes)
- ½ large spring onion (scallion), roots trimmed
- 1 tablespoon white sugar
- 1 teaspoon minced garlic
- 1 teaspoon coarse sea salt
- 500 g (1 lb 2 oz) tteokbokki-tteok (cylindrical rice cakes see Notes), fresh, defrosted or frozen

Seasoning sauce

- 4 tablespoons gochugaru (Korean chilli flakes)
- 3 tablespoons white sugar
- 2 tablespoons jin ganjang (Korean soy sauce)
- 2 tablespoons gochujang (Korean chilli paste)
- 2 tablespoons oyster sauce
- 1 teaspoon vegetable oil
- ½ teaspoon finely ground black pepper

1 In a small bowl, combine all the seasoning sauce ingredients. Mix well until a smooth paste forms, then set aside.

2 Cut the eomuk sheets in half, then into triangles. Cut the spring onion lengthways in half, then into 4–5 cm (1½–2 inch) lengths.

3 Heat a wok over medium–high heat. Add the spring onion to the dry wok and saute for 1–2 minutes, until slightly fragrant.

4 Add the eomuk and 600 ml (20½ fl oz) water, then add the sugar, garlic and salt. Cover the wok and bring the mixture to the boil.

5 Add the rice cakes and boil for about 2 minutes if they are fresh or defrosted (or 4–5 minutes if cooking the rice cakes from frozen), so they start to soften and absorb some of the broth.

6 Remove the lid, add the seasoning sauce and stir well to coat everything with the sauce. Continue to boil, uncovered, for another 4 minutes, stirring frequently, until the rice cakes are tender and chewy and the sauce has thickened to your desired consistency.

7 Ladle into bowls and enjoy immediately as a delicious and spicy Korean street food dish!

Notes

Used in soups and street foods, eomuk are processed seafood products made by blending ground white fish (such as pollock or cod) with flour or starch, seasonings and sometimes vegetables. The mixture is shaped – most commonly into thin, rectangular sheets – and then boiled or deep-fried until firm. You will find packets of eomuk in the refrigerated section of Korean supermarkets.

Tteokbokki-tteok are thick, cylindrical rice cakes used for this dish. Their sturdy shape is perfect for absorbing the spicy sauce while maintaining a satisfyingly chewy texture. Look for them in vacuum-packed bags in the refrigerated or frozen sections of Korean supermarkets.

JEYUK-BOKKEUM

STIR-FRIED SPICY PORK

Often affectionately called 'men's soul food', this fiery, flavourful stir-fried pork dish really packs a punch. It's a wildly popular lunch choice for office workers, and an unbeatable anju (drinking snack) on a night out. Spicy, savoury and slightly sweet, it perfectly captures the bold and dynamic flavours Koreans crave.

SERVES 2

- 350 g (12½ oz) pork shoulder, sliced about 3 mm (⅒ in) thick (see Note)
- vegetable oil, for stir-frying
- 1 spring onion (scallion), sliced diagonally
- 1 white onion, sliced lengthways
- ½ carrot, cut into half-moons about 1 cm (½ in) thick
- ground black pepper, to taste
- sesame oil, for drizzling
- toasted sesame seeds, for sprinkling

Marinade

- 70 ml (2¼ fl oz) jin ganjang (Korean soy sauce)
- 2 tablespoons gochujang (Korean chilli paste)
- 2 tablespoons gochugaru (Korean chilli flakes)
- 2 tablespoons oligo syrup
- 2 tablespoons mirim (Korean cooking rice wine)
- 1 tablespoon white sugar
- 1 tablespoon minced garlic
- 1 teaspoon minced ginger

1 In a bowl, combine all the marinade ingredients. Mix well until a smooth sauce forms.

2 Place the pork slices in another bowl, gently separating any that are clumped together. Add the marinade and, using your hands, thoroughly mix the pork with the marinade, ensuring every piece is well coated. Cover and refrigerate for at least 3 hours, or preferably overnight for the best flavour.

3 Heat a wok over high heat until it's very hot. Add 1 tablespoon vegetable oil and the spring onion. Stir-fry over medium heat for about 3 minutes to infuse the oil.

4 Add the marinated pork, onion and carrot. Reduce the heat to medium-low and stir-fry for 5–7 minutes, allowing the moisture from the pork and vegetables to evaporate. Continue stir-frying for a further 5–10 minutes, until the pork is mostly cooked through and the vegetables are tender-crisp.

5 Once most of the moisture has evaporated, increase the heat to high and quickly stir-fry for another minute. This quick, high-heat stir-fry helps the sauce to stick to the meat and vegetables, enhancing the flavour.

6 Sprinkle with a little black pepper, then transfer to serving plates. Drizzle with sesame oil, sprinkle generously with sesame seeds and enjoy hot, with warm freshly cooked rice (see pages 186 or 188). Kimchi, fresh ssam (see page 128) and mildly flavoured side dishes such as Gyeran-mari (rolled omelette, page 26) and Gim gui (toasted seaweed sheets, page 178) would also be great accompaniments.

Note

You can buy pork shoulder already sliced for jeyuk-bokkeum at Korean grocery stores, which is a convenient option. If you're slicing the pork yourself from a whole shoulder, there is a perfect trick to get those thin, even slices: just place the pork in the freezer for 30–60 minutes prior to slicing. This will firm up the meat just enough to make it easy to slice very thinly with a sharp knife, giving you the perfect texture for a quick stir-fry.

DAKGALBI

SPICY STIR-FRIED CHICKEN

Get ready for an interactive feast with this famous spicy stir-fried chicken dish from the city of Chuncheon, about 90 kilometres (56 miles) from Seoul. Cooked right at your table on a sizzling hot plate, this flavourful medley of chicken, vegetables and gochujang sauce is incredibly addictive. The truly Korean way to finish? Stir-frying rice directly into the leftover savoury sauce – a delicious, unmissable experience!

SERVES 2

- 600 g (1 lb 5 oz) boneless chicken thighs or breasts
- 1 tablespoon mirim (Korean cooking rice wine)
- vegetable oil, for stir-frying
- 100 g (3½ oz) wombok (Chinese cabbage), cut into bite-sized pieces
- ½ white onion, sliced lengthways about 1 cm (½ in) thick
- ½ carrot, sliced into half-moons about 1 cm (½ in) thick
- 10 pieces of tteokbokki-tteok (cylindrical rice cakes; see Notes, page 55) (optional)
- 1 spring onion (scallion), sliced diagonally
- toasted sesame seeds, for sprinkling

Marinade

- 60 ml (¼ cup) jin ganjang (Korean soy sauce)
- 2 tablespoons gochujang (Korean chilli paste)
- 2 tablespoons gochugaru (Korean chilli flakes)
- 2 tablespoons mirim (Korean cooking rice wine)
- 1 tablespoon oligo syrup
- 1 tablespoon white sugar
- 1 tablespoon minced garlic
- finely ground black pepper, to taste

1 Cut the chicken into bite-sized cubes. Place in a bowl, sprinkle with the mirim and mix gently to coat. Leave to marinate for 5 minutes.

2 In a separate bowl, combine the marinade ingredients. Mix well until a smooth sauce forms.

3 Add the marinade to the chicken and mix well, ensuring all the chicken pieces are evenly coated. Cover and leave to marinate in the fridge for at least 30 minutes.

4 Heat a wok over medium heat. Add a drizzle of vegetable oil. Add the marinated chicken and begin to stir-fry, reducing the heat to medium-low if the sauce starts to burn. If it seems too dry or is sticking, add a small amount of water (1–2 tablespoons) to prevent burning. Cook slowly for about 10 minutes, turning now and then, until the chicken is about 80 per cent cooked through.

5 Add the cabbage, onion, carrot and rice cakes, if using. Add a small amount of water (2–3 tablespoons) to help the vegetables cook. Mix together well and continue to stir-fry for 5–10 minutes, until the cabbage is tender, and the sauce has reduced and thickened.

6 Add the spring onion and stir-fry for another minute or two, until the spring onion is tender-crisp.

7 Transfer to a serving platter, sprinkle with sesame seeds and serve with warm freshly cooked rice (see pages 186 or 188). Kimchi and mildly flavoured side dishes such as Gyeran-mari (rolled omelette, page 26), Gyeranjjim (steamed egg custard, page 133) and Gim gui (toasted seaweed sheets, page 178) would also be lovely accompaniments.

TANGSUYUK

SWEET AND SOUR PORK

Diving into Korea's favourite Chinese-style dish, prepare to enter a heated debate: 'bumuk' (pour the sauce) or 'jjikmuk' (dip the sauce)? While its origins are Chinese, this crispy sweet-and-sour pork dish has been thoroughly adopted and adapted by Koreans, becoming a highly popular choice for family gatherings and celebrations. This classic Korean-Chinese dish is enjoyed as a shared centrepiece to complement noodle dishes such as Jjajangmyeon (Korean-Chinese black bean noodles, page 75) or jjamppong (spicy seafood noodle soup).

SERVES 4

- 6 dried wood ear mushrooms
- 380 g (2 cups) potato starch
- 600 g (1 lb 5 oz) pork loin, cut into 4–5 cm (1½–2 in) long batons
- 1 tablespoon mirim (Korean cooking rice wine)
- ½ teaspoon fine sea salt
- ¼ teaspoon finely ground black pepper
- 1 egg white, beaten
- vegetable oil, for deep-frying

Sauce

- 120 ml (4 fl oz) jin ganjang (Korean soy sauce)
- 120 ml (4 fl oz) rice vinegar
- 1 tablespoon tomato ketchup
- ½ carrot, sliced into 5 mm (¼ in) half-moons
- ½ white onion, cut into 2 cm (¾ in) chunks
- ½ short cucumber, sliced into half-moons
- 80 g (½ cup) fresh or tinned pineapple chunks
- 1 tablespoon potato starch, mixed to a slurry with 2 tablespoons water

Notes

It's best to make the sauce while the pork is frying. Because the sauce contains cornflour, it will become very thick as it cools, making it difficult to pour over the pork.

You should only add the vegetables and the cornflour slurry to the simmering sauce base just before you're ready to serve. This ensures the sauce is warm, glossy and at the perfect consistency when you pour it over the crispy pork and the wood ear mushrooms.

1 Place the dried mushrooms in a bowl, cover with warm water and leave to soak for about 20 minutes. Once rehydrated, drain well, slice into quarters and set aside.

2 Meanwhile, place the potato starch in a large bowl, pour in 500 ml (2 cups) water and stir well. Leave to sit for at least 10 minutes, to allow the starch to settle to the bottom and separate from the water.

3 Place the pork in another large bowl. Evenly sprinkle with the mirim, salt and pepper and mix until well coated. Leave to marinate for 10 minutes, then mix the egg white through.

4 Carefully discard all the separated clear water from the top of the potato starch batter. Add only the thick, paste-like starch sediment from the bottom of the bowl to the pork. Mix thoroughly, ensuring the pork is evenly coated all over with the thick starch batter.

5 Pour about 750 ml (3 cups) vegetable oil into a wok or deep-fryer. Heat the oil until it reaches 160°C (320°F), or until a cube of bread dropped in the oil browns in 30–35 seconds.

6 Using tongs, and working in batches, carefully hold each piece of batter-coated pork in the hot oil for about 5 seconds before releasing it. Fry over medium heat for 5–7 minutes, until the exterior is crispy and the pork pieces float to the top, and any that have stuck together detach themselves naturally. Transfer to a wire rack to drain the excess oil, then repeat with the remaining pork.

7 For an extra crispy texture, turn the oil temperature up and fry the pork pieces again at 170°C (340°F) for 2–3 minutes, until they turn a beautiful golden-brown colour, then drain again on a wire rack.

8 Meanwhile, to make the sauce, combine the jin ganjang, rice vinegar and ketchup in a small saucepan. Stir in 360 ml (12 fl oz) water and bring to the boil over medium heat. Add the carrot, onion, cucumber, pineapple and the rehydrated wood ear mushrooms and simmer for just a couple of minutes, until tender-crisp rather than soft. This is key to the dish's texture. Slowly pour the potato starch slurry into the boiling sauce, stirring continuously until the sauce reaches your desired thickness.

9 Tangsuyuk can be served in two ways: either pour the sauce directly over the fried pork, or serve the sauce on the side for dipping, allowing the pork to retain its crispness until eaten. Enjoy hot!

MANDU

DUMPLINGS

Filled with vegetables, meat or kimchi, these delightful dumplings are a highlight of Seollal (Korean Lunar New Year), where families traditionally gather to make them. There's even a fun superstition: beautifully shaped mandu are said to bring beautiful daughters!

You can easily customise the filling to suit your personal preferences or dietary requirements. For gluten-free dumplings, for example, simply use gluten-free soy sauce, oyster sauce and dumpling wrappers.

For vegetarian dumplings, or chae mandu, simply use the vegetable filling and be sure to use a vegetarian mushroom-based oyster sauce, or substitute the oyster sauce with more soy sauce and a pinch of sugar. For a vegan version, omit the egg from the vegetable filling, and ensure your dumpling wrappers are egg-free; you can also increase the amount of tofu, or add mushrooms or other finely julienned vegetables.

The filling for gogi mandu (meat dumplings) is primarily minced pork combined with the chae mandu vegetable filling.

Kimchi is the star of kimchi mandu, which is made by adding kimchi to the chae mandu vegetable base. (But please note that the kimchi filling isn't used in vegetarian dumplings because kimchi is not vegetarian.)

MAKES AROUND 40

40 round dumpling wrappers

Choganjang (vinegared soy sauce, page 195), to serve

Vegetable base filling (for chae mandu)

200 g (7 oz) mung bean sprouts

80 g (2¾ oz) dangmyeon (Korean sweet potato starch noodles)

250 g (9 oz) firm tofu

100 g (3½ oz) Korean chives (see Note) or garlic chives, sliced

120 ml (4 fl oz) jin ganjang (Korean soy sauce)

2 eggs, lightly beaten

2 tablespoons oyster sauce

2 tablespoons sesame oil

2 tablespoons potato starch

½ teaspoon ground black pepper

Meat filling (for gogi mandu)

250 g (9 oz) minced (ground) pork

1 tablespoon mirim (Korean cooking rice wine)

1 tablespoon minced garlic

½ teaspoon minced ginger

½ teaspoon fine sea salt

¼ teaspoon ground black pepper

1 × quantity vegetable base filling (above)

Kimchi filling (for kimchi mandu)

½ head well-fermented kimchi, about 400 g (14 oz)

5 tablespoons gochugaru (Korean chilli flakes)

1 × quantity vegetable base filling (above)

To make the vegetable base filling

1 Blanch the mung bean sprouts in boiling water for about 1 minute. Immediately rinse under cold water, then squeeze out as much water as possible. Chop into 1 cm (½ in) pieces and place in a very large mixing bowl.

2 Cook the noodles in a large saucepan of boiling water for 7–8 minutes, until soft and chewy. Rinse under cold running water and drain well. Chop finely and add to the mixing bowl.

3 Place the tofu in a clean tea towel or piece of muslin (cheesecloth) and squeeze out as much excess water as possible. Finely crumble the tofu with your hands and add to the mixing bowl.

4 Add the remaining filling ingredients and mix thoroughly by hand until well combined. This filling will keep in a sealed, airtight container in the fridge for 1–2 days.

To make the meat filling

1 In a mixing bowl, marinate the minced pork with all the other ingredients. Mix well and set aside for 15 minutes to tenderise the pork and to remove any gamey odour.

2 Add the pork mixture to the vegetable base filling and mix thoroughly by hand until well combined.

To make the kimchi filling

1 Finely chop the kimchi. Place in a clean tea towel or piece of muslin (cheesecloth) and squeeze out all the excess liquid.

2 Add the kimchi and gochugaru to the vegetable base filling. Mix thoroughly by hand until well combined.

Continues next page →

Note

Known as buchu, Korean chives have flat, long leaves and a strong, pungent flavour that is a cross between onion and garlic.

To make the dumplings

1 Lay a dumpling wrapper flat on the palm of your hand. Lightly moisten all around the edge of the wrapper with water using your finger.

2 Place about a teaspoon of your chosen filling in the centre of the wrapper. (The most important thing is to use an amount that allows you to seal the dumpling properly without any filling bursting out!) Fold the bottom edge of the wrapper over the filling to create a half-moon shape, pressing firmly around the edges to seal the dumpling and remove any trapped air. Repeat with the remaining filling and dumpling wrappers.

3 The dumplings will keep for a day or two in an airtight container in the fridge. For longer storage, freezing is the best option – first place them on a baking tray or large plate, leaving space in between, and freeze for 1–2 hours, until the dumplings are completely solid. Once frozen, transfer to a freezer-safe bag or container and freeze for up to 3 months. When cooking frozen dumplings, do not thaw them – just cook them directly from the freezer.

To cook the dumplings

1 Half-fill a large saucepan with water and bring to a rolling boil over high heat. Working in batches, arrange the dumplings in a steamer basket lined with perforated baking paper, ensuring the dumplings don't touch each other.

2 Cover the basket and steam for 15 minutes, or until the wrappers are translucent and the filling is cooked through.

3 Enjoy hot, with choganjang on the side for dipping.

BIBIMBAP

MIXED RICE WITH VEGETABLES

Bibimbap means 'mixed rice' in Korean (bibim means mixing, while bap means rice). It's a colourful and nourishing dish made by serving various seasoned vegetables, meat (often beef), a fried egg and spicy chilli paste over a bowl of warm rice, drizzled with a hint of sesame oil to help bring out all the flavours. Bibimbap is widely loved for its visual appeal, nutritional balance, and the freedom to customise ingredients based on season, diet or personal preference.

While different versions of bibimbap exist all over Korea, the city of Jeonju is widely celebrated as the birthplace of its most famous and refined style – so much so that bibimbap is widely considered a must-eat for anyone visiting the area.

Ultimately, the spirit of bibimbap is to create a colourful and delicious bowl using a variety of ingredients, so feel free to get creative with whatever you have on hand, to achieve a pleasing texture and flavour profile. To replace the fibrous texture of gosari (fern bracken), for instance, you can use stir-fried zucchini (courgette), which adds a delicious soft crunch and sweetness to the bowl. Similarly, if you can't find doraji (bellflower root), which is known for its satisfying crunch, mung bean sprouts are a perfect substitute, as they're already a very common bibimbap ingredient. Any of the seasoned vegetables from the Samsaek namul recipe on page 40 will also make a wonderful bibimbap addition.

SERVES 4

- 200 g (7 oz) doraji (bellflower root; see Note)
- 200 g (7 oz) dried gosari (fern bracken), soaked overnight to remove bitterness
- 300 g (10½ oz) spinach
- vegetable oil, for pan-frying
- fine sea salt
- 200 g (7 oz) carrot, julienned
- 10 fresh shiitake mushrooms, thinly sliced
- 4 eggs
- 740 g (4 cups) warm cooked white rice (Bap, page 186)

Quick pickled radish kimchi

- ½ small white radish, peeled and julienned
- 1 tablespoon coarse sea salt
- 1 tablespoon white sugar
- 1 tablespoon gochugaru (Korean chilli flakes)
- ½ teaspoon rice vinegar
- 1 teaspoon sesame seeds, fresh or toasted

To serve

- Yakgochujang (seasoned chilli paste, page 193)
- toasted sesame seeds
- sesame oil

Note

Doraji, or bellflower root, is a root vegetable with a distinctive crunchy texture and a slightly bitter, earthy flavour. In Korean grocery stores, it's most often sold conveniently pre-prepared, shredded and vacuum-packed. Doraji has been used as a medicinal herb in Korea since ancient times, to help reduce inflammation and for bronchial health.

Koreans love to eat a lot of vegetables in their bibimbap, but you can halve the doraji and gosari quantities if you prefer.

1 Peel the doraji and soak in water for 30 minutes to remove the bitterness.

2 Meanwhile, prepare the quick pickled radish kimchi. Place the radish in a bowl, sprinkle with the salt and leave to sit for 10–15 minutes. Squeeze out the excess moisture, then mix with the remaining pickle ingredients. (This pickle is best served just after you make it, to keep its signature crunch. While it will still be delicious after a day or two in the fridge, the radish will begin to soften and release water, and the flavours will intensify.)

3 Bring a large saucepan of water to the boil, add the drained rehydrated gosari and cook for 5–10 minutes, or until soft. Rinse under cold running water, trim off the tough stems and cut into bite-sized pieces. Set aside.

4 Blanch the spinach in boiling water for 30 seconds, then rinse under cold water and squeeze out the excess water. Set aside.

5 Drain the soaked doraji. Heat 1 teaspoon vegetable oil in a frying pan, add the doraji and stir-fry over medium heat for about 5 minutes, until tender-crisp. The goal is to cook it just enough to slightly soften it, while still maintaining its signature crunchy texture; be careful not to overcook the doraji, or it will lose its unique bite. Lightly season with salt, remove from the pan and set aside.

6 Wipe the pan clean. Lightly saute the blanched gosari in the frying pan with 1 teaspoon vegetable oil over medium heat for 3–5 minutes, until the gosari becomes very fragrant and takes on a soft, tender-chewy texture without losing its shape. Season with a pinch of salt, remove from the pan and set aside.

7 Wipe the pan clean again. Separately stir-fry the carrot and shiitake mushrooms in a little more oil over medium heat until tender. Season with a pinch of salt and set aside.

8 Lightly oil a large non-stick frying pan over medium-low heat. Gently crack the eggs into the pan and let them cook for 2–3 minutes for sunny side up. The eggs are ready when the whites are fully set, but the yolks are still bright and runny.

9 To assemble the bibimbap, place the warm cooked rice in serving bowls. Neatly arrange each of the prepared vegetables around the rice in an aesthetically pleasing colour combination, placing a fried egg in the centre.

10 Add a spoonful of yakgochujang paste, sprinkle with toasted sesame seeds and drizzle with a bit of sesame oil. Mix well before eating!

SPAM KIMCHI BOKKEUM-BAP

SPAM KIMCHI FRIED RICE

Got some leftover rice and tangy kimchi in the fridge? Then you're just minutes away from the ultimate leftover revival, kimchi bokkeum-bap. This incredibly popular and satisfying fried rice dish is the perfect solution for turning older 'troublesome' fermented kimchi that's too sour to enjoy as a fresh side dish into a delicious meal. Simply stir-fry it with rice – and, for the ultimate combo, add some savoury Spam or leftover barbecue pork and top with a perfectly fried egg. This easy, hearty and endlessly customisable dish is a comforting staple in Korean homes, proving that humble leftovers can create an absolute flavour explosion!

It's best to use day-old or cooled rice to achieve a fluffy, non-soggy texture.

SERVES 2

- vegetable oil, for stir-frying
- ½ large spring onion (scallion), thinly sliced
- 200 g (7 oz) tin Spam, cut into small bite-sized cubes
- 200 g (7 oz) well-fermented kimchi, chopped (see Note)
- 80 ml (⅓ cup) kimchi juice
- 1 tablespoon white sugar
- 2 teaspoons gochugaru (Korean chilli flakes)
- 2 tablespoons jin ganjang (Korean soy sauce)
- 300 g (10½ oz) leftover cooked white rice (cooled for best texture)
- 2 eggs
- 1 tablespoon sesame oil
- sesame seeds, for sprinkling

Note

If using kimchi that is less fermented and sour, add 2 teaspoons vinegar during cooking.

1 Heat 60 ml (¼ cup) vegetable oil in a wok or large frying pan. Add the spring onion and saute over low heat for a minute or two to infuse the oil.

2 Add the Spam and cook, stirring frequently, until nicely browned and crispy on all sides.

3 Add the kimchi and kimchi juice and saute for 5–10 minutes, until the kimchi softens.

4 Stir in the sugar and gochugaru. Continue to cook, stirring, for 3–5 minutes, to balance the kimchi's sourness and enhance its savoury flavour.

5 Push the ingredients to one side of the wok, creating an empty space. Pour the jin ganjang directly onto the hot exposed surface of the wok. Let it bubble intensely for a few seconds to develop a rich, slightly smoky 'fire taste', then quickly mix it into the other ingredients. This step enhances the umami flavour.

6 Add the cooled cooked rice to the wok. Break up any clumps of rice, tossing and stirring to ensure the rice is evenly coated with the seasonings and ingredients. Stir-fry for a further 10 minutes, until everything is well combined and heated through.

7 While the fried rice is cooking, heat a little vegetable oil in a small non-stick frying pan. Gently crack the eggs into the pan and let them cook for 2–3 minutes for sunny side up. The eggs are ready when the whites are fully set, but the yolks are still bright and beautifully runny.

8 Taste the fried rice and season with salt and pepper if needed. Drizzle with the sesame oil for aroma.

9 Scoop the rice into two serving bowls. Top with the fried eggs, sprinkle with sesame seeds and enjoy straight away.

A WORLD OF NOODLES

Korean cuisine boasts an array of noodles, each with its own texture and flavour, perfect for any mood or season.

More than just a simple dish, noodles are a beloved staple, offering comfort in the middle of winter, refreshment on a hot summer day or a satisfyingly spicy kick whenever the mood strikes. Each type of noodle has its own distinct characteristics, from the type of flour used to make them, to their shape and common flavour pairings.

It might surprise you to hear, but on a scorching summer day in Seoul, nothing is more perfect than a bowl of cold noodles. In Korea there is debate over the best simple bowl of cold noodles – do you prefer Pyongyang-pa or Hamheung-pa? But I'm not one to take sides – I just eat both!

Pyongyang naengmyeon is a masterpiece of subtlety. Originating from Pyongyang, the capital of North Korea, the dish's charm lies in a clear, beef-based broth with a refreshingly mild flavour. For some, its quiet beauty is the ultimate taste of purity, but for others, it's an acquired taste. When I'm craving the clean, refreshing flavour of Pyongyang naengmyeon, I head straight to the historic Woo Lae Oak restaurant – it's the oldest active Pyongyang naengmyeon restaurant in Seoul.

Hamheung naengmyeon is the vibrant counterpart. This recipe was brought to Seoul by refugees from Hamgyong province during the Korean War. It features thin, incredibly chewy noodles often made from sweet potato starch. Instead of a mild broth, the noodles are typically mixed with a spicy, gochujang-based sauce for a bold and invigorating kick. Whenever I'm in the mood for something spicy and chewy, I seek out Ojangdong Hamheung Naengmyeon.

Mul naengmyeon (cold buckwheat noodle soup, page 69) is another cold noodle dish that Seoulites adore, it's the ultimate summer refresher. These very thin, long and exceptionally chewy noodles are served in an icy, tangy broth (which can be made from beef, or beef and radish water kimchi). The unique chewy texture and exhilaratingly cold, savoury and tangy broth offer instant relief from sweltering summer heat.

Bibim-guksu (spicy noodles, page 70) is another popular warm-weather noodle dish. These thin, chewy wheat noodles are tossed in a vibrant, spicy gochujang-based sauce and typically mixed with fresh vegetables. It is a fantastic option for those who love a spicy kick and a lighter, but still flavourful, meal.

If you're looking for a bowl of noodles to keep you warm during the winter months, a bowl of Kalguksu (homemade knife-cut noodle soup, page 126) might be just what you need. Kalguksu is almost always served in a comforting, hot broth, which can be seafood-based (using anchovy or clam broth), chicken-based, or even mushroom-based. Often accompanied with seasonal vegetables like zucchini and potatoes, it's true homemade comfort in a bowl.

When I'm craving a truly authentic and bustling Seoul food experience, I head straight to Namdaemun Kalguksu Alley. It's one of my favourite spots in the city – a stretch of small, no-frills eateries where you sit elbow-to-elbow with locals. What I love most about this alley is the incredible variety on offer and it is always great value. It's a delicious and wonderfully communal experience that truly captures the energy of the city.

MUL NAENGMYEON

COLD BUCKWHEAT NOODLE SOUP

Mul naengmyeon is a perfectly refreshing dish for scorching summer days... yet this iconic cold noodle dish was originally considered a winter delight! In the chilly northern regions of Korea, during the bitterly cold winters people would gather in rooms made toasty with underfloor heating (ondol) and slurp down icy-cold buckwheat noodles in a frosty dongchimi (water radish kimchi) broth – a truly exhilarating contrast.

But the story gets even more intriguing! Naengmyeon may just be the world's first recorded delivery food. Back in the 18th century, vendors would transport this cold noodle dish to customers, carefully preserving its icy temperature.

SERVES 2

- 2 × 300 ml (10 fl oz) packets of store-bought naengmyeon broth – either beef- or dongchimi (water radish kimchi)-based
- 300 g (10½ oz) buckwheat noodles (see Note)
- ½ short cucumber, cut into thin matchsticks
- 1 boiled egg, cut in half lengthways

To serve

- rice vinegar
- Korean hot yellow mustard
- toasted sesame seeds

1 Place the broth packs in the freezer for at least 30 minutes before serving, or until the liquid inside is very cold and has started to solidify to a slushy consistency.

2 Bring a large saucepan of water to a rolling boil. Add the noodles and cook according to the packet directions – typically 2–3 minutes. Be sure not to overcook the noodles, so they don't lose their texture.

3 Strain the noodles and rinse thoroughly under cold running water, rubbing them gently with your hands to remove the excess starch. Drain well.

4 Arrange the noodles in two large shallow serving bowls. Pour the icy cold broth over the noodles.

5 Garnish with the sliced cucumber and egg halves and serve immediately, with the rice vinegar, mustard and sesame seeds on the side.

Note
Koreans love to eat a large portion of noodles in their mul naengmyeon, but you can halve the quantity of buckwheat noodles if you would prefer a less substantial meal.

BIBIM-GUKSU

SPICY NOODLES

This vibrantly spicy cold noodle dish harks back to times of rice shortages, when wheat-flour noodles became a much-loved staple. Tossed in a sweet, spicy and tangy gochujang sauce and finished with fresh vegetables, it's a simple but refreshing and invigorating meal. For the best flavour, prepare the sauce the day before.

SERVES 4

- 400 g (14 oz) somyeon (thin wheat noodles)
- 4 green lettuce leaves, shredded
- 1 short cucumber, cut into thin matchsticks
- 2 hard-boiled eggs, cut in half lengthways
- toasted sesame seeds, for sprinkling
- sesame oil, for drizzling

Sweet spicy sauce

- 80 ml (⅓ cup) rice vinegar
- 60 ml (¼ cup) maesil cheong (green plum extract)
- 2 tablespoons white sugar
- 3 tablespoons gochujang (Korean chilli paste)
- 1 tablespoon jin ganjang (Korean soy sauce)
- 2 teaspoons minced garlic
- 1½ teaspoons gochugaru (Korean chilli flakes)

1 To make the sauce, combine the vinegar, maesil cheong and sugar in a small bowl. Stir well until the sugar is mostly dissolved, then add the remaining ingredients and mix thoroughly until well combined. Cover and marinate in the fridge overnight, if possible, for a deeper flavour.

2 Bring a large saucepan of water to a rolling boil. Gently spread the noodles as you add them to the boiling water, then stir them with chopsticks to prevent sticking. When the water begins to foam and boil up to the rim of the pan, add 125 ml (½ cup) cold water. Continue to boil for about 4 minutes, until the noodles start to float to the surface.

3 Strain the noodles and rinse thoroughly under cold running water, rubbing them gently with your hands to remove the excess starch. Drain well.

4 Transfer the noodles to a large clean bowl. Add the sauce and toss gently but thoroughly to evenly coat the noodles with the sauce.

5 Divide the noodles among serving bowls, then top with the lettuce, cucumber and egg halves. Sprinkle generously with sesame seeds, drizzle with a little sesame oil and serve immediately.

갈아만든
배

연겨자

RAMYEON

KOREAN INSTANT NOODLES

More than just a meal, ramyeon is a cultural phenomenon in Korea, a symbol of the nation's rapid post-war development and convenience. What began as a quick, affordable meal has evolved into a customisable comfort food that is endlessly experimented with. This is a basic recipe but you can adapt it as you wish. Some popular additions for a heartier meal include Kong namul (seasoned bean sprouts, page 40), Mandu (dumplings, page 58), and sliced tteok (rice cakes). You can also add a slice of cheese for a savoury richness, or crack in a raw egg for a creamier broth. A final garnish of thinly sliced spring onion (scallion) is the perfect finishing touch to enhance the flavours and aroma.

SERVES 1

1 packet of your favourite Korean instant noodles

1 egg

1 Check your noodle packet and pour the recommended quantity of water into a small saucepan. (Some Koreans prefer to use slightly less water than recommended for a more concentrated and flavourful broth.) Bring to a rolling boil over high heat.

2 Once boiling, add the powdered soup mix and dried vegetable flakes from the noodle packet. Let the water come back to the boil.

3 Carefully place the block of instant noodles into the boiling water, then cook for the time specified on the packet – usually 3–4½ minutes. To get that perfect chewy texture Koreans prefer, lift and drop the noodles repeatedly with your chopsticks during cooking; this exposes them to air and helps them cook more evenly.

4 About 1–2 minutes before the noodles are done, add the egg. If you prefer it soft-boiled, crack the egg directly into the boiling broth – but don't stir if you want a runny yolk. If you prefer whipped egg, lightly beat the egg first and, about 30 seconds before serving, slowly pour it into the boiling broth while stirring gently, for a more integrated, cloudy egg texture.

5 Transfer to a serving bowl and enjoy!

JJAJANG-MYEON

KOREAN-CHINESE BLACK BEAN NOODLES

In Korea, jjajangmyeon is more than just comfort food – it's tied to some of life's biggest moments. On graduation day, it's a child's first dining out experience, marking a step into adulthood. When moving house, it's the first meal shared in a new home, often delivered in iconic metal boxes.

Adapted from Chinese zhajiangmian by early immigrants, jjajangmyeon has become a cherished part of Korean culture; thick noodles in a rich black bean sauce, they're the taste of celebration and nostalgia.

SERVES 4

- 3 tablespoons vegetable oil
- 120 g (4½ oz) chunjang (Korean black bean paste)
- 200 g (7 oz) pork loin, cut into 1.5 cm (½ in) cubes
- 1 large onion, cut into 1.5 cm (½ in) cubes
- 1 potato (about 150 g/5½ oz), peeled and cut into 1.5 cm (½ in) cubes
- ½ zucchini (courgette), cut into 1.5 cm (½ in) cubes
- 200 g (7 oz) wombok (Chinese cabbage), cut into 1.5 cm (½ in) cubes
- 500 ml (2 cups) water or vegetable stock
- 1 tablespoon white sugar
- 1 tablespoon oyster sauce
- 2 tablespoons potato starch
- 4 × 250 g (9 oz) servings of fresh Korean jjajangmyeon noodles, or thick udon noodles

Garnishes (optional)

- julienned cucumber
- 2 hard-boiled eggs, cut in half lengthways

1 Heat a wok or large saucepan over medium heat. Add the vegetable oil. Once hot, add the chunjang and fry for 3–5 minutes, stirring constantly, until very fragrant and glossy. This process removes the raw, bitter taste from the black bean paste and develops its rich flavour. Carefully scoop the paste into a bowl, leaving the excess oil in the pan.

2 Add the diced pork to the wok. Stir-fry over medium-high heat for 3–5 minutes, until the pork is cooked through and lightly browned.

3 Add the onion and potato and stir-fry for 3–5 minutes, until the onion is translucent and the potato begins to soften.

4 Add the zucchini and cabbage and stir-fry for another 2–3 minutes, until the zucchini and cabbage are slightly tender but still have some crunch.

5 Add the fried black bean paste and mix thoroughly, ensuring all the ingredients are well coated with the paste. Stir-fry for another 1–2 minutes.

6 Pour in the water or stock, then stir in the sugar and oyster sauce and bring back to a simmer.

7 Mix the potato starch with 80 ml (⅓ cup) water until smooth, then add the starch water to the simmering sauce, stirring continuously. Continue stirring until the sauce thickens to your desired consistency, then simmer for another 1–2 minutes to cook out the starch taste.

8 While the sauce is simmering, bring a large saucepan of water to a rolling boil. Add the noodles and cook until al dente. Fresh noodles typically cook quickly (2–4 minutes).

9 Drain and rinse the noodles thoroughly to remove the excess starch and stop them sticking together, then drain well again.

10 Divide the noodles among serving bowls. Generously spoon the pork mixture over the noodles. Garnish with cucumber and/or an egg half, if desired, and serve.

JAPCHAE

STIR-FRIED GLASS NOODLES AND VEGETABLES

Traditionally served during holidays and celebrations such as New Year's Day (Seollal) and the Harvest Festival (Chuseok), and for special occasions such as birthdays and parties, japchae is prized for its chewy texture, colourful ingredients and crowd-pleasing taste.

SERVES 8 AS A SIDE DISH

- 6 dried wood ear mushrooms
- 200 g (7 oz) pork shoulder, thinly sliced
- vegetable oil, for stir-frying
- 1 white onion, julienned
- ½ carrot, julienned
- ½ red bell pepper (capsicum), julienned
- ½ yellow bell pepper (capsicum), julienned
- 4 fresh shiitake mushrooms, julienned
- 200 g (7 oz) spinach
- fine sea salt
- 300 g (10½ oz) dangmyeon (Korean sweet potato starch noodles)
- 3 tablespoons white sugar
- 140 ml (4½ fl oz) jin ganjang (Korean soy sauce)
- 1 tablespoon minced garlic
- 2 tablespoons sesame oil
- sesame seeds, for sprinkling

Marinade

- 1 tablespoon jin ganjang (Korean soy sauce)
- 1 tablespoon sesame oil
- 2 teaspoons minced garlic
- 2 teaspoons white sugar
- 1 teaspoon mirim (Korean cooking rice wine)
- pinch of ground black pepper

1 Place the dried mushrooms in a bowl, cover with warm water and leave to soak for about 20 minutes. Once rehydrated, drain well, cut into quarters and set aside.

2 Meanwhile, combine all the marinade ingredients in a bowl. Add the pork and mix well, then leave to marinate for about 15 minutes.

3 Lightly oil a large, non-stick frying pan or wok. Working in separate batches to preserve each ingredient's individual flavour, texture and colour, stir-fry the onion, carrot, bell peppers, wood ear mushrooms, shiitake mushrooms and spinach over medium heat for 1–2 minutes each, seasoning each batch with a pinch of salt during cooking. The onion, carrot and bell peppers should be tender but still crisp, and the mushrooms and spinach should be wilted. Remove each batch from the pan and set aside.

4 Using the same pan, stir-fry the pork over medium heat for about 10 minutes, until fully cooked. Set aside.

5 Meanwhile, cook the noodles in a large saucepan of boiling water for 7–8 minutes, until soft and chewy. Drain thoroughly, removing the excess water, to help the noodles absorb the seasoning better. Toss the drained noodles with a little vegetable oil to stop them sticking together.

6 While the noodles are still warm, place them in a large mixing bowl. Add the sugar first, then the soy sauce and garlic. Mix well so the flavours absorb evenly. Add the stir-fried vegetables and pork, drizzle with the sesame oil and gently toss.

7 Clean out the pan or wok and reheat with a little oil over medium-low heat. Lightly stir-fry the noodles, vegetables and pork together one last time for a deeper flavour.

8 Garnish with toasted sesame seeds and serve warm.

DOENJANG JJIGAE

SOYBEAN PASTE STEW

If kimchi is the heart of Korean cuisine, then doenjang jjigae is its soul. This humble stew – made with aged soybean paste, vegetables and tofu – has been simmering in Korean kitchens for generations. Served bubbling hot in earthenware pots known as ttukbaegi, it's an everyday dish that captures the warmth, simplicity and depth of Korean home cooking.

If using a traditional Korean earthenware pot, be aware that it retains heat exceptionally well. If the stew ingredients, especially the chilli flakes, appear to be burning during the sauteing process, you can temporarily turn off the heat and let the residual heat continue cooking the stew before turning the heat back on.

SERVES 2

- 400 ml (14 fl oz) Anchovy-kelp broth (page 192)
- 2 tablespoons doenjang (Korean soybean paste), plus extra to season
- 2 small potatoes, peeled and cut into 2 cm (¾ in) cubes
- ½ white onion, peeled and cut into 2 cm (¾ in) cubes
- ⅓ zucchini (courgette), cut into 2 cm (¾ in) half-moons
- 2 fresh shiitake mushrooms, cut into 2 cm (¾ in) chunks
- 150 g (5½ oz) firm tofu, cut into bite-sized chunks
- 1 teaspoon minced garlic
- 1 teaspoon gochugaru (Korean chilli flakes)
- ⅓ large spring onion (scallion), thinly sliced diagonally
- 1 green chilli, thinly sliced diagonally
- 1 red chilli, thinly sliced diagonally
- guk ganjang (Korean soup soy sauce) or yeondu (fermented bean essence), to taste (optional)

1 Pour the anchovy broth into a small saucepan or Korean earthenware pot. Using a fine-mesh sieve, press the doenjang through the sieve into the broth to ensure it dissolves smoothly without lumps.

2 Bring the broth to a rolling boil over high heat, then reduce the heat to medium. Add the potato and onion, cover the pot and leave to simmer for 5 minutes, or until the potato is about half-cooked.

3 Add the zucchini, mushrooms, tofu, garlic and gochugaru. Simmer for another 3 minutes, allowing the flavours to meld and the vegetables to cook through.

4 Finally, add the spring onion and the green and red chilli. Stir gently and cook for 1–2 minutes, until the spring onion softens slightly.

5 Taste the stew and, if it seems bland, add a touch more doenjang, or a small amount of guk ganjang or yeondu to adjust the seasoning if needed.

6 Serve hot, with warm rice (see pages 186 or 188) on the side .

100%

DWAEJIGOGI KIMCHI JJIGAE

PORK KIMCHI STEW

When Koreans crave warmth and spice, they turn to kimchi jjigae, a bubbling stew that embodies the heart of Korean home cooking. Featuring aged kimchi simmered with pork or tofu, its spicy, tangy and deeply savoury flavours are incredibly comforting. It's the quintessential soul-warming dish, perfect for any cold day.

SERVES 4

- 300 g (10½ oz) pork shoulder, cut into bite-sized chunks
- 2 tablespoons mirim (Korean cooking rice wine)
- 600 g (1 lb 5 oz) well-fermented kimchi
- 2 tablespoons vegetable oil
- 1 tablespoon minced garlic
- 2 tablespoons jin ganjang (Korean soy sauce)
- 2 tablespoons gochugaru (Korean chilli flakes)
- 2 teaspoons white sugar
- ½ onion, sliced about 1 cm (½ in) thick
- 1 spring onion (scallion), sliced diagonally
- 300 g (10½ oz) firm tofu, cut into bite-sized cubes
- 1 tablespoon tuna extract (chamchi-aek), or to taste

1 Place the pork in a bowl and drizzle with 1 tablespoon of the mirim. Mix to coat, then leave to marinate for at least 10 minutes. This helps tenderise the meat and remove any gamey odours.

2 Remove and discard the tough inner core from the kimchi head. Cut the rest of the kimchi into bite-sized pieces, about 3 cm (1¼ in) in length. Set aside, reserving 100 ml (3½ fl oz) of the kimchi juice to add later.

3 Heat the vegetable oil in a saucepan or Korean earthenware pot. Add all the pork and saute over medium heat for 5–10 minutes, until the pork is mostly cooked. Once some of its fat has rendered, push the pork to one side of the pan, add the garlic and saute for another minute or two, until fragrant.

4 Add the jin ganjang directly onto the hot exposed surface of the pan, avoiding the pork. Let the liquid sizzle and slightly caramelise for a few seconds to develop a deeper aroma.

5 Reduce the heat to low. Add the gochugaru and stir continuously to infuse the sauce and prevent burning, creating a fragrant chilli oil base.

6 Add the chopped kimchi and sugar. Cook over medium-low heat for 5–10 minutes, until the kimchi becomes translucent and softens, stirring occasionally to prevent sticking.

7 Pour in 1 litre (4 cups) water and the reserved kimchi juice. Increase the heat to high and bring to a rolling boil, then reduce the heat to medium.

8 Add the onion and spring onion. Cover and simmer for at least 30 minutes to allow the broth to develop and the flavours to deepen.

9 Add the tofu, then simmer for another few minutes to allow the tofu to absorb the stew's flavours.

10 Taste the stew and season as needed with the tuna extract. Serve hot and bubbling, with warm freshly cooked rice (see pages 186 or 188).

SUNDUBU JJIGAE

SOFT TOFU STEW

Experience the silken comfort of sundubu jjigae, a vibrant, spicy nourishing stew overflowing with impossibly soft tofu. Often served bubbling hot in a traditional earthenware pot, this Korean staple is a popular choice for its soothing texture, gentle yet flavourful warmth and customisable spice level.

SERVES 2

- 1 tablespoon vegetable oil
- ½ spring onion (scallion), sliced
- 1 tablespoon minced garlic
- 1 tablespoon gochugaru (Korean chilli flakes)
- 1 tablespoon guk ganjang (Korean soup soy sauce), plus extra to serve
- 600 ml (20½ fl oz) Anchovy-kelp broth (page 192)
- 400 g (14 oz) soft tofu or silken tofu (see Note), cut into 2 cm (¾ in) thick rounds or large chunks
- ½ white onion, cubed
- ⅓ zucchini (courgette), cut into 2 cm (¾ in) thick half-moons
- 1 tablespoon tuna extract (chamchi-aek)
- 1–2 eggs
- 100 g (3½ oz) enoki mushrooms
- fine sea salt (optional)

1 In a small saucepan or earthenware pot, heat 1 tablespoon vegetable oil over medium-low heat. Add the spring onion and garlic and saute for a minute or two, until the spring onion softens slightly and the mixture is fragrant.

2 Reduce the heat to low. Add the gochugaru and stir constantly for 3–5 minutes, to allow the chilli oil to infuse without burning.

3 Push the aromatics to one side and pour the guk ganjang directly onto the hot exposed surface of the pot. Allow to sizzle briefly and develop a deeper flavour, then stir it into the mixture.

4 Pour in the anchovy broth and bring to the boil over medium heat.

5 Add the tofu, onion and zucchini. Note that soft tofu releases a lot of water, which can dilute the seasoning, so be prepared to adjust before serving.

6 Add the tuna extract and leave to simmer vigorously for about 10 minutes, until the vegetables are tender.

7 Crack the eggs directly into the pot and immediately turn off the heat. (The residual heat from the pot will cook the egg white, while leaving the yolk beautifully runny.) Add the mushrooms.

8 Taste the stew and adjust the seasoning as needed with more guk ganjang or a pinch of fine sea salt. Serve bubbling hot, with warm freshly cooked rice (see pages 186 or 188).

Note

Korean soft tofu is often sold in a plastic tube. To remove it, carefully cut the tube in half horizontally. Gently squeeze or pull the end to carefully slide the tofu out without breaking it.

짜릿함은 그대로,
칼로리는 제로!
Chilsung Cider
롯데칠성
Coca-Cola

농축수산물
ILHO
46
호
현이네
010-8336-3088
동일유통
TERRA

SAMGYETANG

GINSENG CHICKEN SOUP

When summer hits its peak in Seoul, locals dive into a steaming hot bowl of samgyetang! This isn't just chicken soup; it's a centuries-old tradition and a unique Korean secret for beating the heat. Samgyetang is a whole young chicken, often stuffed with ginseng, sticky rice, jujube dates and garlic, then slow-simmered to tender perfection. It's a deeply nourishing, aromatic bowl designed to invigorate the body and restore energy – a fascinating summer ritual based on the ancient concept of Iyeolchiyeol, meaning 'to fight heat with heat'.

For an authentic presentation, serve each diner's soup in an individual earthenware pot. The sizzling earthenware pot is placed in the centre of a table setting that also includes chopsticks, a soup spoon, a small dish of salt and pepper, and small banchan (side dishes), especially Kkakdugi (diced radish kimchi, page 172), to cut through the richness of the soup.

To eat it, use chopsticks to pull the tender meat from the bone and dip it into the salt and pepper and enjoy. Then, use a spoon to scoop up the savoury broth and the chapssal (glutinous rice) that has cooked inside the chicken. The rice, soaked in the rich broth, becomes a delicious, porridge-like part of the feast – a complete and incredibly comforting meal, all in one pot.

SERVES 2

- 200 g (1 cup) glutinous rice
- 2 whole young chickens, 500–600 g (1 lb 2 oz–1 lb 5 oz) each
- 10 whole garlic cloves, peeled
- 6 dried Korean jujube dates (see Note)
- 2 pieces fresh or dried ginseng (each approx. 7–8 cm/ 2¾–3¼ in)
- 1 teaspoon whole black peppercorns
- 1 spring onion (scallion), plus extra thinly sliced spring onion to garnish
- fine sea salt, to serve
- finely ground black pepper, to serve

1 Soak the rice in a bowl of water for 1 hour. Drain thoroughly.

2 Remove the tail fat from each chicken, to remove any gamey odours. Under cold running water, gently scrape and wash away any red blood clots from the surface and inside the cavity of each chicken. Trim and remove the tips of the wings.

3 Carefully stuff each chicken cavity with half the soaked glutinous rice, 3 or 4 whole garlic cloves, 3 jujubes and 1 piece of ginseng. Do not overstuff the chickens, as the rice will expand.

4 Use kitchen string to tie the chicken legs together, to secure the cavity and prevent the stuffing falling out during cooking. (Alternatively, make a small slit on the skin of one chicken thigh near the end, then thread the end of the other chicken leg through this slit.)

5 Place both stuffed chickens, breast side up, in a stockpot or large deep saucepan. Add the peppercorns, spring onion and the remaining garlic cloves. Pour in 2 litres (2 quarts) water and bring to a rolling boil over high heat.

6 Reduce the heat to medium–low, cover and gently simmer for 1 hour, occasionally skimming off any foam or impurities that rise to the surface to ensure a clear and clean broth.

7 To serve, preheat two earthenware pots on the stovetop (one for each chicken) until the pots feel warm to the touch; this only takes 2–3 minutes.

8 Carefully transfer one cooked chicken to each earthenware pot. Pour enough hot broth over each chicken so it is about two-thirds submerged. Bring the pots to a gentle simmer on the stove, which should only take 3–5 minutes.

9 When the broth begins to bubble around the edges and the pots themselves are hot enough to continue bubbling at the table, carefully transfer the pots to the table. Garnish the soups with the thinly sliced spring onion and serve immediately, with a small dish of salt and pepper for dipping the chicken pieces into.

Note

Jujubes are a type of date that are usually sold dried, and are red or dark red in colour. They are about the size of a thumb; generally, the bigger the date, the better the quality.

SEOLLEONG-TANG

OX BONE SOUP

The secret to this restorative and deeply comforting soup lies in the long simmering of the beef bones and brisket. It requires some patience, but it's worth it for a bowl of soup that is sure to warm your body and soul. This milky-white ox bone soup is so deeply rooted in Seoul's history that one of the oldest seolleongtang restaurants has been granted Seoul Future Heritage status as a cultural treasure worthy of preservation.

This soup is classically served with kkakdugi (diced radish kimchi), for the perfect balance of flavours and texture.

MAKES 3 LITRES (3 QUARTS) BROTH; SERVES 4–5

2.5 kg (5½ lb) beef bones
600 g (1 lb 5 oz) beef brisket

To serve

200–250 g (7–9 oz) cooked thin wheat noodles
sliced cooked beef brisket
thinly sliced spring onion (scallion) rounds, white part only
fine sea salt, to taste
ground black pepper, to taste

1 Place the beef bones in a very large pot and cover completely with cold water. Leave to soak for at least 6 hours to draw out impurities and blood, changing the water every hour to keep it clean. This crucial step ensures a clear and less 'gamey' broth.

2 Drain the bones. Fill a clean stockpot with fresh water and bring to a rolling boil. Add the beef bones and boil vigorously for 10–15 minutes. This step helps remove any remaining impurities and scum.

3 Carefully discard all the cooking water. Thoroughly rinse each bone, as well as the beef brisket, under cold running water, scrubbing off any remaining scum, bone fragments and blood spots. Clean the stockpot as well.

4 Place the cleaned bones and beef brisket in the stockpot. Add about 5 litres (5 quarts) fresh water, ensuring the bones and meat are fully submerged. Bring the water to a strong boil over high heat, then reduce the heat to medium-low and simmer gently for 1 hour.

5 Carefully remove the brisket from the broth and wrap tightly in plastic wrap to stop the beef drying out as it cools. (Once cooled, set aside in the fridge, to make it easier to cut, then slice against the grain for garnishing the soup; the beef itself is traditionally served cold.)

6 Meanwhile, allow the bones and broth to simmer gently for a further 2 hours.

7 After 3 hours of simmering, strain the entire contents of the pot through a fine-mesh sieve, into another large saucepan or container, reserving the broth. Discard any remaining small bone fragments. Carefully separate any tender meat and tendons from the bones; these can be reserved as additional soup toppings.

8 Return only the strained bones to the clean stockpot. Add enough fresh water - 2–3 litres (2–3 quarts) - to completely submerge the bones again. Bring to the boil over high heat, then reduce the heat to medium–low and simmer for another 4–5 hours, or until the broth turns a milky white colour. Throughout this long simmering process, use a ladle to regularly skim off any fat or impurities that rise to the surface.

9 Strain the broth again through a fine-mesh sieve, then leave to cool completely. Once cold, a layer of solidified fat will form on top; carefully remove and discard this fat layer for a clear broth.

10 Combine this second batch of broth with the first batch of broth (reserved from step 7). This combined broth can be stored in airtight containers or vacuum-sealed bags in the fridge for 3–4 days, or frozen (in convenient individual portion sizes) for up to 3 months.

11 When ready to serve, pour about 700 ml (23½ fl oz) of the broth per serve into an earthenware pot and bring to a rolling boil.

12 Portion 50 g (1¾ oz) cooked noodles per serving bowl, then ladle the broth over the top. Arrange the cold beef brisket slices on top, garnish with spring onion and serve with salt and black pepper at the table, for diners to season their soup to their personal taste. Kkakdugi (diced radish kimchi, page 172) and warm freshly cooked rice (see pages 186 or 188) are traditional accompaniments.

GOGUMA MATTANG

CANDIED SWEET POTATO

Both crispy and chewy, this beloved Korean snack or dessert is yet another delightful example of how simple ingredients can be transformed into a truly satisfying treat.

SERVES 4

4 sweet potatoes, 600–800 g (1 lb 5 oz–1 lb 12 oz) in total, peeled and cut into irregular chunks

vegetable oil, for deep-frying

black sesame seeds, to garnish

Syrup

3 tablespoons white sugar

2 tablespoons vegetable oil

2 tablespoons oligo syrup

pinch of fine sea salt

1 Place the sweet potatoes in water for about 15 minutes, to remove some of the excess starch.

2 Rinse under cold running water, then thoroughly pat dry with paper towel. It's crucial to remove all the moisture to prevent the hot oil splattering during deep-frying.

3 Pour about 2.5 cm (1 in) vegetable oil into a wok or large saucepan (enough oil to fully submerge the sweet potato pieces). Heat the oil to 170°C (340°F), or until a cube of bread dropped in the oil browns in 20 seconds.

4 Carefully add half the sweet potato chunks to the hot oil. Fry for about 5 minutes, until golden brown and cooked through, turning occasionally. Transfer to a wire rack to drain the excess oil, then repeat with the second batch.

5 Place all the syrup ingredients in a small saucepan over low heat. Do not stir the sugar before it melts completely, as this can cause it to crystallise.

6 Once the sugar is completely melted and small bubbles start bubble vigorously, add the fried sweet potato chunks. Gently toss and stir to evenly coat them with the glossy syrup.

7 Finally, add 1 tablespoon water and stir quickly; this helps to create a slightly crispier coating.

8 Transfer to a clean tray, spreading the coated sweet potato chunks out to stop them sticking together.

9 As soon as the sweet potato has cooled and the syrup has hardened, sprinkle with black sesame seeds. Enjoy fresh and warm, while the candied coating is still crisp, before it becomes too tough to eat.

GILGEORI EUMSIK & BUNSIK

SEOUL'S STREET FOOD

Seoul's streets pulsate with energy, and much of that comes from its vibrant street food culture, which is known as 'gilgeori eumsik'.

From bustling markets to small carts tucked away on side streets, gilgeori eumsik provides a sensory feast of sizzling sounds, enticing aromas and colourful displays of these quick, delicious and often incredibly affordable bites. It's the perfect fuel for busy commuters, a beloved after-school treat for students and a popular late-night snack for friends catching up and unwinding.

Myeongdong Street is a famous street food spot in Seoul, but you can also find great options at the Gwangjang and Tongin markets. Gwangjang market has to be my favourite Korean street food destination, it's the best place to feel the vibrant energy of Seoul. I love sitting among the crowds enjoying a wide variety of authentic dishes.

Whenever I'm at Gwangjang market I love grabbing some mayak gimbap, small, addictive bite-sized rice rolls that are served with a tangy mustard sauce on the side. Then, I head to the main food alley to grab a freshly fried bindaetteok, a savoury mung bean pancake that is crispy on the outside and soft on the inside. To top it all off, I finish with a warm, sweet Hotteok (syrup-filled sweet pancake, page 96) or a crispy Kkwabaegi (twisted doughnut, page 99).

A very significant and beloved style of street food is bunsik, which literally means 'food made from flour' and broadly refers to the popular snack foods like Ramyeon (Korean instant noodles, page 73), Tteokbokki (stir-fried rice cakes, page 51) and breads. These dishes are the go-to choices for Seoulites who want a casual meal, a quick bite or a late-night indulgence. Many bunsik restaurants and street stalls offer a lively, no-frills dining experience, perfect for a quick and flavourful pick-me-up.

Here are some of the most iconic and beloved bunsik and gilgeori eumsik you'll find in Seoul:

Tteokbokki (page 51)

This iconic stir-fried rice cake dish is considered by many to be the soul of bunsik culture. Mabokrim Grandma's Tteokbokki is located in the heart of the famous Sindang-dong Tteokbokki Town. This legendary spot is a must-visit for anyone who has fallen in love with these chewy rice cakes. This place specialises in tableside tteokbokki (called jeukseok tteokbokki). You cook the rice cakes and other ingredients right at your table in a communal hot pot, creating a fun and authentic dining experience.

Hot dog (page 95)

The beloved Korean corn dog features a crispy, slightly sweetened batter that can sometimes be coated with French fries. They can be filled with sausage or even mozzarella cheese for a delightful cheesy pull. Myungrang Hot Dog branches are everywhere in Korea and they are great places to try this adored snack – their cult-favourite 'Myungrang Dog', which comes with various coatings and fillings, is a great way to fuel up on a night in the capital.

Ramyeon (page 73)

This instant noodle dish is a staple in Korean homes, but ramyeon served at bunsik restaurants or street stalls is elevated with extra ingredients like egg, cheese or vegetables, creating a comforting and quick meal. The Jongno 24 Hours Ramen Convenience Store is a self-service ramyeon shop where you can cook your favourite Korean instant ramyeon whenever you like.

Patbingsu (page 100)

A refreshing shaved ice dessert, particularly popular in the summertime. It's usually topped with sweet red beans, tteok (rice cakes) and condensed milk, and sometimes with fruit or ice cream. To experience the full spectrum of patbingsu available in Seoul you should try the two very different styles – traditional and modern.

Dongbinggo is famous for its simple yet traditional patbingsu, where the quality of the shaved ice and the flavour of the sweet red beans are the stars.

If you're looking for a modern, creative twist on the classic, Bubing is the spot. They offer a wide range of unique flavours and toppings beyond the traditional red bean (think strawberry, black sesame, sweet corn and more), appealing to those who want a more contemporary and Instagram-worthy dessert.

소떡소떡
2,500
수제 핫도그
2,000
떡꼬치
2개 1,000
쏘세지
2,000
오뎅
2개 1,000
1개 700
쌀 진공 떡볶이
쌀 진공 떡볶이

HOT DOG

KOREAN CORN DOGS

Forget what you know about hot dogs! The Korean hot dog is a street food sensation with a fascinating twist. While its roots are American, the iconic Dongdaemun-style hotdog is a playful, textural and wildly popular snack that often comes on a stick, coated in a doughy deep-fried batter! For a traditional Korean street food experience, you can roll the hot dogs, fresh from the fryer, in white sugar, giving them a generous coating, then serve with a good drizzle of your favourite sauces, such as ketchup, mustard or even a spicy chilli sauce.

MAKES 10

- 10 hot dog sausages
- 1 litre (4 cups) vegetable oil, for deep-frying
- 150 g (5½ oz) panko breadcrumbs

Dough batter

- 250 ml (1 cup) lukewarm water
- 2 teaspoons instant dried yeast (7 g sachet)
- 1 egg, lightly beaten
- 300 g (2 cups) plain (all-purpose) bread flour
- 2 teaspoons fine sea salt
- 4 tablespoons white sugar

Notes

Another popular variation is to make cheesy hot dogs using half sausage and half cheese. To do this, cut five hot dog sausages and five string cheese sticks or mozzarella sticks in half, crossways, so you have 10 fat sausage chunks and 10 cheese chunks. Thread a sausage chunk, then a cheese chunk, onto each of your 10 wooden skewers, then batter and fry the dogs as directed.

Or, instead of hot dogs, make cheesy dogs! Omit the sausages altogether and just thread 10 string cheese sticks or mozzarella sticks onto 10 wooden skewers, then batter and fry the dogs as directed.

1 Start by making the batter. Pour the lukewarm water into a sealable container, add the yeast and mix well until dissolved. Add the sugar and stir again, then stir the beaten egg through.

2 Sift the flour into the wet ingredients. Using a sturdy rubber spatula, mix together until no dry spots of flour remain, and a soft, shaggy dough forms.

3 Cover the container securely and place in a warm spot. Leave to rise for 1–1½ hours, until the dough has visibly doubled in size.

4 Gently press down on the dough with your hands to release the gases. Using your rubber spatula, lightly fold the dough over itself a few times to smooth it out. Cover again and leave to rise for another 30 minutes.

5 When ready to start cooking, thread each sausage onto a wooden skewer.

6 Pour the vegetable oil into a deep saucepan or deep-fryer. Heat the oil until it reaches 160°C (320°F), or until a cube of bread dropped in the oil browns in 30–35 seconds.

7 Holding a skewered sausage with your hand, dip the sausage into the dough batter and gently rotate the skewer about one and a half full rotations, to evenly wrap the dough around the entire sausage.

8 Roll the dough-coated hot dog evenly and thoroughly in the breadcrumbs.

9 Carefully place the hot dog in the hot oil. Fry for about 5 minutes, until golden brown and crispy, turning occasionally for even cooking. Transfer to a wire rack to drain any excess oil.

10 Repeat with the remaining hot dogs and serve immediately, while fresh and hot.

HOTTEOK

SYRUP-FILLED SWEET PANCAKES

Indulge in the irresistible warmth of this popular Korean winter street snack. These crispy and chewy pancakes are a delightful cold-weather treat, perfectly embodying the cosy spirit of Korean street food.

MAKES 6

- 180 ml (6 fl oz) lukewarm water
- 60 ml (¼ cup) lukewarm milk
- 50 g (1¾ oz) white sugar
- 2 teaspoons instant dried yeast (7 g sachet)
- 30 ml (1 fl oz) vegetable oil, plus extra for pan-frying
- 240 g (8½ oz) plain (all-purpose) flour
- 60 g (2 oz) glutinous rice flour
- ½ teaspoon fine sea salt

Filling

- 100 g (3½ oz) light brown sugar
- 30 g (1 oz) chopped mixed nuts (walnuts, peanuts and/or sunflower seeds recommended)
- 1 teaspoon ground cinnamon

1 In a large bowl, combine the water, milk, sugar and yeast. Stir gently and leave to sit for about 5 minutes, until the yeast starts to foam up.

2 Add the 30 ml (1 fl oz) vegetable oil to the yeast mixture.

3 In a separate bowl, whisk together the plain flour, rice flour and salt.

4 Add the flour mixture to the wet ingredients, mixing with a rubber spatula until a sticky dough forms.

5 Cover the bowl tightly with plastic wrap, then leave to rise in a warm place for 1 hour, or until the dough has roughly doubled in size.

6 Once the dough has risen, combine all the filling ingredients in a small bowl, mixing well.

7 Lightly oil your hands (to help prevent sticking) and gently punch down the dough to release the gas. Divide the dough into six equal portions, then roll each portion into a ball.

8 Take one dough ball in the palm of your hand and flatten it into a disc shape. Spoon 1½–2 tablespoons of the filling into the centre. Carefully gather the edges of the dough and pinch them together tightly at the top to completely seal the filling, to prevent any sugar spilling out during cooking. Repeat with the remaining dough and filling.

9 Heat a large frying pan over medium heat and add a generous drizzle of vegetable oil. Working in batches, carefully place several filled dough balls in the pan, sealed side down, making sure they are not sticking to each other. Cook for 30 seconds to 1 minute, until lightly golden underneath.

10 Flip the dough balls over, then press down firmly using a flat spatula, to flatten each one into a round pancake 1–1.5 cm (½ in) thick. But be careful not to press so hard that the filling spills out!

11 Cook for about 5 minutes, until the second side is golden brown and crispy, and the filling inside is melted and gooey.

12 Remove from the pan and serve immediately. Be careful while eating as the sugar filling will be very hot and syrupy!

KKWABAEGI

TWISTED DOUGHNUTS

Meet kkwabaegi, Korea's beloved twisted doughnut. While this popular treat is now considered a simple, comforting street snack, similar twisted doughnuts were once served on royal tables. These are an especially nostalgic snack for many Koreans.

MAKES 15

275 ml (9½ fl oz) milk, at room temperature
60 g (2 oz) white sugar
3 teaspoons (10 g) instant dried yeast
1 large egg, at room temperature, beaten
400 g (2⅔ cups) white bread flour
150 g (5½ oz) glutinous rice flour
1½ teaspoons salt
30 g (1 oz) unsalted butter, at room temperature
vegetable oil, for deep-frying

Coating

1 teaspoon ground cinnamon
110 g (½ cup) white sugar

1 In a large bowl, combine the milk, sugar and yeast. Stir gently to dissolve the yeast, then add the egg and stir lightly to combine.

2 Add the bread flour, rice flour and salt and mix using a spatula until a shaggy dough forms and no dry bits of flour are visible. Once the dough comes together, rub in the butter.

3 Knead the dough by hand for 10–15 minutes, until it becomes smooth and elastic. Shape the dough into a smooth ball, cover the bowl with plastic wrap, and leave to rise in a warm place for 1 hour, or until the dough has doubled in size.

4 Gently remove the dough from the bowl and press down to release the gas. Divide the dough into 15 equal portions, each weighing about 60 g (2 oz). Roll each portion into a smooth ball.

5 Arrange the dough balls on a tray, ensuring they don't stick together. Cover with a damp clean towel or plastic wrap, so they don't dry out. Rest on the bench for 15–20 minutes.

6 Using both hands, gently roll a dough ball into a rope 25–30 cm (10–12 in) long. For the last few rolls, move one hand upward and the other downward so that the dough begins to build tension and twist.

7 Pick up the rope, holding one end in each hand, and bring the ends together. The dough should begin to twist on itself as it hangs, but you can twist the dough once or twice more to accentuate the twists if need be. Pinch the ends firmly to seal. Repeat with the remaining dough portions.

8 Arrange on a baking tray lined with baking paper, spacing them well apart. Cover lightly with plastic wrap or a damp towel and leave to rise for another 40 minutes, or until doubled in size.

9 Pour 5–10 cm (2–4 in) vegetable oil into a deep saucepan or deep-fryer (enough oil to allow the doughnuts to float freely). Heat the oil to 170–175°C (340–345°F), or until a cube of bread dropped in the oil browns in about 20 seconds.

10 Combine the coating ingredients on a wide tray or plate.

11 Working in batches, carefully lower several doughnuts into the hot oil, ensuring there is plenty of room for them to float freely. Fry for 1–2 minutes, until the dough turns a deep golden brown, then flip and fry the other side for about 30 seconds, until golden.

12 Transfer to a wire rack set over a tray to briefly drain the excess oil. While still warm, roll them in the coating mixture and serve immediately.

PATBINGSU

SHAVED ICE WITH RED BEAN TOPPING

Beat the heat the Korean way with this delightfully refreshing shaved ice dessert! Traditionally piled with sweet red beans, patbingsu has evolved into a dazzling, customisable treat – think mountains of finely shaved ice topped with an incredible array of fresh fruits, condensed milk, or even green tea. You'll find these indulgent creations everywhere, from cosy cafes to luxurious hotel lounges. It's the perfect cool-down on a hot Seoul day, offering endless flavour fun. You will need a shaved ice machine for this recipe (see Note).

SERVES 4

ice cubes, for shaving

Red bean paste

250 g (1 cup) dried red beans
220 g (1 cup) white sugar
pinch of salt

Toppings

mini rice cake balls (patbingsu-tteok)
sweetened condensed milk
roasted soybean powder

Note
If you don't have a shaved ice machine, you can crush ice in a blender. For a fluffier result, freeze a mixture of milk and sweetened condensed milk overnight in ice cube trays, then simply blend the frozen cubes until they have a soft, snowy texture.

1 Rinse the dried beans thoroughly under cold running water. Place in a saucepan and add enough fresh water to completely submerge them. Bring to a rolling boil over high heat, then boil for about 5 minutes. This first blanching helps remove bitterness and impurities from the beans. Discard the blanching water and lightly rinse the beans again.

2 Return the blanched beans to the same pan and cover with enough fresh water to completely submerge the beans. Bring to the boil, then reduce the heat to low and simmer gently for about 40 minutes, or until the beans are very soft and easily mashable.

3 Reduce the heat to medium-low, add the sugar and salt and continue to simmer for 5–10 minutes, stirring frequently, until the mixture thickens to a jam-like consistency.

4 Remove from the heat and leave to cool completely. Refrigerate in an airtight container until ready to use.

5 When ready to serve, place a serving bowl under a shaved ice machine. Fill the machine with ice cubes and shave the ice into the bowl until you have a good mound of shaved ice flakes (about 2 cups). Repeat with the remaining serving bowls.

6 Generously scoop the sweet red beans (about 1 large spoonful per serving) over the shaved ice. Top each with the mini rice cake balls, drizzle each generously with condensed milk (around 2 tablespoons per serve is recommended) and finish with a generous sprinkling of roasted soybean powder. Enjoy immediately.

LATE

포장 가능
TAKE OUT
₩5,000
TTEOK
BOKKI
SOJU ₩6,000
BEER ₩3,000
₩8,000

예일치과 의원
신속히 이동하여
노래방
2F
성신아트컬렉션
성수 연세 의원 3F
돼지네
GS25
연무장5가길

Seoul's skyline may dim after midnight, but its kitchens don't. Yasik means 'food eaten in the middle of the night after dinner', and locals order it as naturally as they check the weather.

A tap on your smartphone can summon anything – from crispy fried chicken to bubbling seafood stews – delivered by scooters that weave through the neon-lit alleyways. Whether you're at home, at a park or even by the Han River, you can easily order almost any kind of food directly to you, often arriving within minutes.

A favourite among Seoulites is chimaek – this combination of fried chicken and beer is arguably the king of Korean late-night food. Tongdak (whole fried chicken), often served crispy and golden, is the perfect companion to an icy cold beer. You can also find variations like spicy Yangnyeom tongdak (Korean-style fried spicy chicken, page 120). Kyochon Chicken is a nationwide chain known for its unique, thinly coated fried chicken. Kyochon's signature is its variety of addictive sauces, with the most famous being the perfectly balanced soy garlic and the sweet and savoury honey flavours.

Jokbal (page 134) and Bossam (wrapped pork with radish kimchi, page 136) are two popular boiled pork dishes that are perfect late-night food. Jokbal is braised pork trotters and bossam uses pork belly, both dishes are often ordered together and the meat is served as a ssam (a delicious parcel of meat wrapped with lettuce or perilla leaves that is served with raw garlic, chilli and ssamjang/seasoned bean paste, page 194 – the essential dipping sauce). Seoul is famous for its food alleys and both jokbal and bossam have alleys named after them where you'll find plenty of vendors who specialise in these quintessential Korean dishes.

Jeon are another favourite to be delivered or ordered at restaurants late at night. These savoury pan-fried pancakes can be made with a variety of meat, seafood, vegetables and other ingredients, meaning there is a whole world of delicious jeon to discover when you visit Seoul! You can read more about jeon on page 106. There are plenty of jeon restaurants in Seoul that specialise in serving a variety of jeon – it's a lot of fun to visit with friends and order a big platter to share!

Korean late-night culture is not just about the food; it's about extending social gatherings, unwinding after a long day and enjoying delicious moments that stretch into the early hours. It's an essential part of the Seoul experience, and these dishes are at its very heart.

JEON

SAVOURY PANCAKES

Get ready to discover jeon, a diverse and utterly delicious world of Korean savoury pancakes. Far more than just a side dish, jeon covers everything from crispy, spicy kimchi-jeon (kimchi pancakes, page 108) and savoury Donggeurang-ttaeng (pork patties, page 111) to the tasty Aehobak-jeon (zucchini pancakes, page 114) and the fragrant, seafood-packed Haemul pajeon (seafood and spring onion pancakes, page 116).

Jeon can be divided into two main types, which have slightly different preparations: pancake style, where ingredients are mixed directly into a flour-based batter and cooked as one large, single pancake; and an egg-coated style, where individual bite-sized morsels (such as small meat patties or zucchini slices) are lightly coated in flour and then dipped in an egg wash before being pan-fried.

Symbolising abundance and celebration, jeon are a staple for Korean holidays such as Seollal (Korean Lunar New Year) and Chuseok, a major mid-autumn harvest festival similar to Thanksgiving, when families gather to celebrate and give thanks for the harvest.

But here's where the story deepens: jeon has a special, almost magical connection with rainy days in Korea! There's a delightful custom of craving and making jeon when the rain falls, often accompanied with a comforting bowl of makgeolli (Korean rice wine). The sizzling sound of the jeon batter hitting the pan is said to mimic the sound of falling rain, creating a perfect sensory experience. It's a heartwarming tradition that truly captures the cosy, communal spirit of Korean life. So, when the skies open up in Seoul, you know exactly what to do!

탄산

KIMCHI-JEON

KIMCHI PANCAKES

These pancakes are particularly savoured for their addictive combination of spicy, tangy, sour kimchi and perfectly crispy batter. They are a classic Korean comfort food famously enjoyed on a rainy day with a bowl of makgeolli (Korean rice wine). It's best to serve these straight from the pan, cut into wedges, with a simple soy-based dipping sauce for the perfect balance of flavours.

MAKES 2 LARGE PANCAKES; SERVES 4 AS AN APPETISER OR SNACK

- 200 g (7 oz) well-fermented kimchi , plus 60 ml (¼ cup) kimchi juice
- 120 g (1 cup) Buchimgaru (Korean pancake mix, page 190)
- 120 ml (4 fl oz) cold water
- vegetable oil, for pan-frying
- Choganjang (vinegared soy sauce, page 195), to serve (optional)
- spring onions (scallions), thinly sliced, to serve (optional)

1 Roughly chop the kimchi into bite-sized pieces, reserving the juice for the batter.

2 Pour the kimchi juice into a large bowl. Add the pancake mix and water and whisk together well, until you have a smooth batter. The consistency should be pourable but slightly thick.

3 Add the chopped kimchi and mix thoroughly to combine.

4 Heat a large non-stick frying pan over medium heat. Add a generous amount of vegetable oil to coat the bottom of the pan.

5 Pour half the batter into the hot pan, spreading it out thinly and evenly into a round shape. Cook for about 5 minutes, until the edges turn golden brown and crispy.

6 Once nicely browned underneath, carefully flip the pancake over. Add a little more oil around the edges to help the other side become crispy. Cook the second side for about 5 minutes, until it's also golden brown and cooked through.

7 Slide the cooked pancake onto a serving plate and repeat with the remaining batter, to make a second pancake.

8 Serve immediately, cut into wedges. The pancakes are delicious on their own, but even better with choganjang as a dipping sauce and sprinkled with spring onions.

Paldo

DONGGEURANG-TTAENG

PORK PATTIES

In English, the name of this dish roughly translates to 'round, flat thing', perfectly describing these delicious little jeon. While 'patty' or 'fritter' are good English descriptions for these small, round delights, in the Korean culinary context, they are considered a meat-based jeon (pancake), as the term 'jeon' refers to any dish that is pan-fried after being coated in flour and egg.

Made from minced meat and vegetables, and celebrated for their soft texture and gentle savoury flavour, these jeon are a holiday favourite and a staple at festive gatherings, adored by all ages for their mild, comforting taste.

MAKES ABOUT 20

- 150 g (5½ oz) firm tofu, crumbled
- 200 g (7 oz) minced (ground) pork
- ¼ onion finely chopped
- ¼ carrot, finely chopped
- ¼ large spring onion (scallion), finely chopped
- 1 tablespoon minced garlic
- 2 large eggs, beaten
- 1 tablespoon mirim (Korean cooking rice wine)
- 1 teaspoon sesame oil
- ½ teaspoon salt
- pinch of ground black pepper
- vegetable oil, for pan-frying
- Choganjang (vinegared soy sauce, page 195), to serve

Coating

- 100 g (3½ oz) Buchimgaru (Korean pancake mix, page 190)
- 1 large egg

1 Place the tofu in a clean tea towel and squeeze out as much excess water as possible. This is important for the patty texture.

2 Place the tofu in a large bowl with the pork, onion, carrot, spring onion and garlic. Add the egg, mirim, sesame oil, salt and pepper. Use your hands to thoroughly mix and knead the mixture until it becomes sticky and cohesive. (Kneading for a few minutes helps the ingredients bind well and results in a better texture.)

3 Take small portions of the mixture – about 30 g (1 oz) each – and roll them into small round balls. Gently flatten them into disc-shaped patties, about 1 cm (½ in) thick.

4 Prepare a coating station by spreading the pancake mix on a plate, and beating the egg in a shallow bowl to make an egg wash.

5 Evenly coat both sides of each patty with the pancake mix, gently shaking off any excess. Dip each floured patty into the egg wash, ensuring it's fully coated.

6 Heat a large non-stick frying pan over medium heat. Add a generous amount of vegetable oil to coat the bottom of the pan.

7 Working in batches, place several patties in the hot pan, ensuring they're not touching each other. Reduce the heat to medium-low and cook for 3–4 minutes on each side, until golden brown and cooked through. Use medium-low heat to ensure the interior cooks through properly without the patties burning.

8 Serve warm, right after frying for the best taste and texture, with choganjang as a dipping sauce.

AEHOBAK-JEON

ZUCCHINI PANCAKES

A simple yet elegant side dish, these jeon are loved for the delicate sweetness and tender texture of the thinly sliced zucchini, highlighting the pure taste of this vegetable. The subtle flavour shines when served warm with a light soy-vinegar dipping sauce, making it a perfect accompaniment to any Korean meal.

MAKES ABOUT 10; SERVES 2

1 zucchini (courgette), sliced into 5 mm (¼ in) thick rounds

½ teaspoon salt

60 g (½ cup) Buchimgaru (Korean pancake mix, page 190)

2 large eggs

vegetable oil, for pan-frying

Choganjang (vinegared soy sauce, page 195), to serve

1 Place the zucchini slices in a bowl and sprinkle with the salt. Leave to sit for 10–15 minutes, to draw out the excess moisture; this prevents the zucchini becoming watery when cooked, and also seasons it lightly.

2 Gently squeeze the zucchini slices or pat them dry with paper towel to remove the released water.

3 Prepare a coating station by spreading the pancake mix on a plate, and beating the eggs in a shallow bowl to make an egg wash.

4 Evenly coat both sides of each zucchini slice with the pancake mix, gently shaking off any excess. Dip each floured zucchini slice into the egg wash, ensuring it's fully coated.

5 Heat a large non-stick frying pan over medium heat. Add a generous amount of vegetable oil to coat the bottom of the pan.

6 Place the zucchini slices in the hot pan and cook for 2–3 minutes on each side, until golden brown and tender.

7 Drain briefly on a plate lined with paper towel and serve warm, with choganjang as a dipping sauce.

HAEMUL PAJEON

SEAFOOD AND SPRING ONION PANCAKES

Pan-fried to golden perfection, with wonderfully crispy edges and a tender, savoury interior, these delightful pancakes are a comforting and popular appetiser or snack and pair perfectly with pickled vegetables. In Korea, this pancake is made with jjokpa, is a type of spring onion that is generally skinnier than conventional spring onions. If they are not available where you live, replace them with the skinniest spring onions you can find.

MAKES 2 LARGE PANCAKES; SERVES 4

- 6 large prawns (shrimp), fresh or frozen (see Note), peeled and deveined
- 200 g (7 oz) mixed seafood (mussels, clams, squid), fresh or frozen (see Note)
- 1 tablespoon rice wine
- 300 g (10½ oz) jjokpa (slender spring onions/scallions)
- 2 large eggs
- 180 g (1½ cups) Buchimgaru (Korean pancake mix, page 190)
- 375 ml (1½ cups) cold water
- vegetable oil, for pan-frying
- 1 red chilli, thinly sliced

To serve (optional)

- Choganjang (vinegared soy sauce, page 195)
- Yachae jangajji (pickled vegetables, page 176)

1 Pat the thawed prawns and seafood dry with a clean tea towel and place in a bowl. Sprinkle with the rice wine and gently mix, then leave to marinate for 5–10 minutes, to help reduce any fishy odours. Drain well, then pat dry with paper towel.

2 Meanwhile, clean and trim the spring onions. Cut them to a length that fits the size of your frying pan - if using a 25 cm (10 in) pan, for instance, cut them to 20–23 cm (8–9 in).

3 In a small bowl, lightly beat the eggs.

4 In a large bowl, whisk together the pancake mix and cold water to form a smooth batter, thick enough to coat the back of a spoon. Add the spring onions and gently toss, ensuring all sides are evenly and thinly coated with the batter.

5 Heat a large non-stick frying pan over medium heat. Add a generous amount of vegetable oil until the surface of the pan is fully covered.

6 Once the oil is hot, arrange about half the battered spring onions evenly in the pan, spreading them out to fill any gaps and form a large, flat layer.

7 Scatter half the seafood over the spring onions, then decoratively arrange half the red chilli slices on top. Ladle about half the beaten eggs evenly over the seafood and spring onions, helping to bind all the ingredients together.

8 Cook over medium heat for 4–5 minutes, until golden brown and crispy underneath. Carefully flip the pancake over and cook the other side for another 3–4 minutes, until the seafood is fully cooked and the pancake is golden brown and crispy. Slide the pancake onto a serving plate.

9 Add more oil to the pan if needed, then repeat with the remaining ingredients to make a second pancake.

10 Serve the warm, crispy pancakes immediately. They are delicious on their own, but even better with a side of choganjang and pickled vegetables.

Note

If using frozen prawns and seafood, thaw them in the fridge overnight. The slow, gradual thawing process keeps the seafood at a safe temperature and helps retain its delicate texture.

TTEOKGALBI

GRILLED SHORT RIB PATTIES

These elegant patties, which originated in Korea's royal court cuisine, feature meat from beef short ribs that has been meticulously minced and shaped into small patties. They are then carefully grilled and glazed for an exquisitely tender banchan (side dish) and are a refined balance of flavour and texture.

MAKES 10 PATTIES

- 650 g (1 lb 7 oz) finely minced beef (preferably short rib meat)
- 2½ tablespoons glutinous rice flour
- 3 tablespoons finely chopped spring onion (scallion), white part only
- vegetable oil, for pan-frying
- toasted sesame seeds, for sprinkling

Seasoning paste

- ¼ Korean pear (or ¼ sweet apple), roughly chopped
- ¼ onion, roughly chopped
- 1 tablespoon minced garlic
- 80 ml (⅓ cup) jin ganjang (Korean soy sauce)
- 2 tablespoons white sugar
- 1 tablespoon oligo syrup
- 2 teaspoons sesame oil
- ½ teaspoon ground ginger
- pinch of ground black pepper

Glaze

- 1 tablespoon jin ganjang (Korean soy sauce)
- 1 tablespoon jocheong (Korean rice malt syrup)
- 1 tablespoon sesame oil
- 1 tablespoon water

1 In a blender, combine all the seasoning paste ingredients, blending until very smooth. (Adding onion and pear to the mix helps tenderise the meat and adds a natural sweetness.)

2 Place the beef in a large mixing bowl. If there's any excess blood, gently pat the meat dry with paper towel.

3 Pour the seasoning paste over the beef, add the rice flour and spring onion and knead the mixture for 5–7 minutes, until smooth and elastic. This process develops the elasticity of the meat, ensuring the patties are tender, juicy and hold their shape well, so they don't fall apart during cooking.

4 Divide the kneaded meat mixture into ten equal portions, weighing about 90 g (3 oz) each. Shape each portion into a round or oval patty, 1.5–2 cm (½–¾ in) thick.

5 In a small bowl, mix the glaze ingredients together until fully combined. This glaze will give the patties a beautiful sheen and an extra layer of flavour during the final grilling.

6 Heat a large non-stick frying pan over medium-low heat. Drizzle in a small amount of vegetable oil. Place the patties in the pan, ensuring there is plenty of space in between them. Cook slowly for 5–7 minutes on each side, to ensure the patties cook through evenly without burning on the outside.

7 Once both sides are browned and the patties are almost cooked through, generously and evenly brush the glaze over both sides of the patties and cook for a further 5 minutes on each side, until thoroughly cooked, glossy and beautifully caramelised.

8 Transfer the hot patties to a serving plate. Sprinkle with toasted sesame seeds and serve immediately with rice (see pages 186 or 188) and side dishes such as kimchi, pickled vegetables such as Yachae jangajji (page 176), Oi muchim (cucumber salad, page 175) and light soups.

YANGNYEOM-TONGDAK

KOREAN-STYLE SPICY FRIED CHICKEN

Get ready to experience Korea's national obsession: fried chicken! This isn't just any fried chicken, but a culinary phenomenon that comes in two irresistible forms: the impossibly crispy original fried chicken (huraideu), and the addictive sweet-and-spicy yangnyeom chicken, both of which you'll discover in the recipe on the following pages.

More than just a meal, fried chicken is a social affair, deeply woven into the fabric of Korean family life and celebrations. For many, it evokes nostalgic memories of childhood, especially as it was famously the celebratory dish eaten on payday (as it used to be quite an expensive meal). It's the ultimate go-to for family gatherings, a night in with friends, or late-night snacks.

In Korea, fried chicken is generally considered a main meal in itself, and is typically served with only a side dish of chicken-mu (pickled radish), offering a refreshing, tangy crunch that perfectly cuts through all the rich flavours.

MAKES ABOUT 10 PIECES; SERVES 2

1.2 kg (2 lb 10 oz) chicken drumsticks

300 g (10½ oz) Korean tempura flour (twigimgaru)

vegetable oil, for deep-frying

Chicken-mu (pickled radish)

500 g (1 lb 2 oz) Korean radish

240 ml (8 fl oz) water

120 ml (4 fl oz) rice vinegar

100 g (3½ oz) white sugar

1 teaspoon fine sea salt

Marinade

1 tablespoon fine sea salt

1 tablespoon mirim (Korean cooking rice wine)

2 teaspoons cayenne pepper

½ teaspoon ground ginger

½ teaspoon onion powder

pinch of black pepper

Chicken-mu

1 Wash the radish thoroughly, then peel and cut into bite-sized cubes. Place in a large heatproof bowl or airtight container.

2 Place the remaining pickle ingredients in a saucepan. Bring to the boil over medium-high heat, stirring occasionally to completely dissolve the sugar and salt.

3 As soon as the liquid boils, turn off the heat and carefully pour the hot pickling liquid over the radish. (The hot liquid will help the radish quickly absorb the flavours and maintain its crispness.)

4 Leave to cool to room temperature, then place the pickle in the fridge for 4 hours or overnight. Chicken-mu is typically enjoyed when the radish is fresh and crunchy. For the best flavour and texture, use within a day or two of making.

Fried chicken

1 Place the chicken drumsticks in a large bowl. Add all the marinade ingredients and mix well, ensuring all the chicken pieces are evenly coated. Cover and refrigerate for at least 4 hours (or overnight for best results), to allow the marinade to penetrate and tenderise the chicken.

Batter

200 g (7 oz) Korean tempura flour (twigimgaru)

1 teaspoon curry powder

1 teaspoon hot paprika

400 ml (14 fl oz) cold water

2 When you're ready to fry the chicken, place the batter ingredients in a large bowl and whisk until smooth and well combined; the consistency should be thin enough to lightly coat the chicken.

3 Place the tempura flour for the dry coating in a large plastic bag.

4 Remove the marinated chicken from the fridge. Dip each drumstick into the batter, ensuring it's coated, but not excessively thick. Let the excess batter drip off, then place the drumsticks in the bag of tempura flour. Holding the bag closed, gently toss and shake the bag until each piece is fully coated with the dry flour. This 'shaking' method helps create that desired wavy, crispy texture in the fried chicken coating.

5 Pour about 7.5 cm (3 in) vegetable oil into a large saucepan or deep-fryer (enough oil to fully submerge the chicken pieces - but ensuring the pan is no more than half-full, so the oil doesn't boil over once the chicken is added). Heat the oil to 170°C (340°F), or until a cube of bread dropped in the oil browns in 20 seconds.

6 Working in batches, carefully lower the coated chicken pieces into the hot oil. For the first 1–2 minutes, do not stir or move the chicken; let the coating set. Moving them too soon can cause the crust to fall off. After 2 minutes, gently separate any chicken pieces that may have stuck together. Continue to fry for another 6 minutes, for a total of 8 minutes for this first frying. Transfer the chicken to a wire rack and leave to drain and rest for 3–5 minutes.

7 Increase the oil temperature slightly to 175–180°C (345–350°F).

8 Working in batches, return the par-fried chicken to the hot oil and cook for another 2 minutes, or until deeply golden brown and exceptionally crispy. Drain again on a wire rack for a minute or two to remove any excess oil, ensuring the coating remains crispy and doesn't become greasy. This is an essential step for achieving that perfect Korean fried chicken texture.

9 Serve half the chicken as is, for the original fried chicken, and generously brush the rest with the spicy yangnyeom sauce. Enjoy immediately, with the refreshingly cold, crunchy chicken-mu.

Continues next page →

Yangnyeom (spicy sauce)

- 125 ml (½ cup) water
- 80 ml (⅓ cup) oligo syrup (or rice syrup or honey)
- 3 tablespoons tomato ketchup
- 2 tablespoons oyster sauce
- 2 tablespoons gochujang (Korean chilli paste)
- 2 tablespoons gochugaru (Korean chilli flakes)
- 2 tablespoons jin ganjang (Korean soy sauce)
- 2 tablespoons white sugar
- 1 tablespoon maesil cheong (green plum extract)
- 1 tablespoon minced garlic

Yangnyeom

1 Combine all the ingredients in a saucepan and bring to a gentle boil over medium heat.

2 Reduce the heat to low and cook for 5–7 minutes, stirring occasionally, until the sauce becomes glossy and thick enough to coat the back of a spoon.

3 If making ahead, transfer to a clean, airtight container; being a cooked sauce with a high sugar and salt content, it will keep in the fridge for 1–2 weeks.

BULGOGI

GRILLED MARINATED BEEF

Literally meaning 'fire meat' in Korean, bulgogi is a dish of thinly sliced meat, typically beef, that is marinated in a flavourful soy-based marinade, then grilled or pan-cooked to bring out its sweet, savoury and slightly smoky taste.

Often served at family gatherings, bulgogi is also popular with foreigners due to its harmony of sweetness and seasonings.

This recipe is a standard bulgogi recipe, but each region in Korea has its own version. In Seoul, the marinated meat is often arranged in a wide, shallow pot with mushrooms and vegetables, then cooked with a significant amount of broth – a type of Korean hot pot known as bulgogi jeongol. This style of cooking creates a bulgogi that is lighter and more like a soup, with a less caramelised flavour than grilled bulgogi. It's often cooked at the table and served family-style.

SERVES 4

- 600 g (1 lb 5 oz) beef sirloin, very thinly sliced (see Note)
- 1 white onion, cut in half, then thinly sliced lengthways
- 1 spring onion (scallion), sliced in half lengthways, then cut into 7.5 cm (3 in) lengths
- 1 tablespoon sesame oil
- toasted sesame seeds, for sprinkling

Marinade

- 120 ml (4 fl oz) jin ganjang (Korean soy sauce)
- 60 ml (¼ cup) mirim (Korean cooking rice wine)
- 2 tablespoons minced garlic
- 2 tablespoons white sugar
- 1 tablespoon maesil cheong (green plum extract)
- ¼ teaspoon ground black pepper

Note
Buying the beef already sliced for bulgogi from a Korean or Asian grocery store is the easiest option. You want the slices to only be about 3 mm (⅒ in) thick. If you can't find the beef pre-sliced or prefer to do it yourself, it is best to put the beef in the freezer for 30–40 minutes, until the meat is firm but not completely frozen. This will make it much easier to get clean, thin slices with a sharp knife.

1 Mix all the marinade ingredients in a large bowl until the sugar is dissolved.

2 Cut the beef slices into smaller bits about 10 cm (4 in) long; they don't need to be perfect squares. The goal is to have pieces of beef that are easy to pick up with chopsticks and that will cook through quickly and evenly.

3 Add the beef to the marinade and mix thoroughly to evenly coat all the slices. Cover and refrigerate for at least 2 hours. For deeper flavour, marinate overnight in the fridge.

4 Heat a large skillet or chargrill pan over medium-high heat. Add the marinated beef, along with the marinade, and stir-fry for 2–3 minutes, until the beef starts to brown and cook through.

5 Add the onion and spring onion and cook for a further 3–5 minutes, stirring occasionally until the onion is tender and the beef is nicely glazed.

6 Turn off the heat and drizzle the sesame oil over the beef mixture. Transfer to a serving plate and garnish with toasted sesame seeds.

7 Serve straight away, with rice (see pages 186 or 188). You can also serve it with Kkakdugi (diced radish kimchi, page 172), Ssam (page 128), Samsaek namul (seasoned vegetables, page 40), Gyeran-mari (rolled omelette, page 26) and Gyeranjjim (steamed egg custard, page 133).

KALGUKSU

HANDMADE KNIFE-CUT NOODLE SOUP

This hearty and warming soup comes in many delicious versions, often featuring a rich broth with vegetables, and sometimes seafood or meat. It's especially cherished on rainy days or during cold weather, feeling like a warm hug. Kalguksu is a truly satisfying and soul-nourishing dish, embodying the simple yet profound comforts of Korean home cooking!

SERVES 2

- 900 ml (30½ fl oz) Anchovy-kelp broth (page 192)
- 1 tablespoon guk ganjang (Korean soup soy sauce)
- ½ teaspoon salt
- ½ onion, julienned
- ¼ zucchini (courgette), julienned
- ¼ carrot, julienned
- ⅓ large spring onion (scallion), sliced diagonally

Noodles

- 240 g (8½ oz) plain (all-purpose) flour, plus extra for dusting
- 160 ml (⅔ cup) warm water (about 40°C/104°F)
- ½ teaspoon fine sea salt

To serve

- Yangnyeom ganjang (seasoned soy sauce, page 195)
- ground black pepper

To make the noodles

1 In a large bowl, combine the flour, water and salt. Use a rubber spatula to stir until the ingredients start to come together. If needed, gradually add 1–2 tablespoons water, until a shaggy dough forms.

2 Turn the dough out onto a clean surface and knead by hand for 10–15 minutes, until the dough is smooth and no longer sticks to your hands or your work surface. This indicates a well-developed dough.

3 Wrap the dough tightly in plastic wrap, or place in a plastic bag. Leave to rest at room temperature for at least 30 minutes to help the gluten relax, making the dough easier to roll.

4 Unwrap the rested dough. To prevent sticking, generously dust your work surface and the dough with extra flour as you roll the dough as thinly as possible using a rolling pin.

5 Once thinly rolled, sprinkle the entire surface of the dough with more flour. Fold the dough in half, then sprinkle more flour on the folded surface, to prevent the layers sticking. Continue folding three or four more times until you have a manageable layered rectangle of folded dough.

6 Using a sharp knife, cut the folded dough into long, thin strips 3–4 mm (⅒–⅙ in) wide. These are your hand-cut kalguksu noodles!

7 Gently unroll and separate each noodle and dust lightly with more flour to stop them sticking together and drying out. If not using straight away, place them in a resealable plastic bag or airtight container and store in the fridge, then used within a day or two for the best texture and flavour. For longer storage, you can freeze the noodles for up to a month, just make sure to defrost them for 15–20 minutes before cooking them.

To make the soup

1 For each serving, prepare about 150 g (5½ oz) of hand-cut noodles. Rinse off any excess starch under running water to ensure a clearer broth. (Noodles with excess starch will make the broth cloudy and thick.)

2 In a saucepan, bring the anchovy broth to the boil over medium heat.

3 Add the noodles and stir gently for 1–2 minutes to stop them sticking together.

4 Season the broth with the guk ganjang and salt. Add the vegetables and continue to cook for about 5 minutes, until the noodles are fully cooked through and the vegetables are tender. When the noodles float to the surface, they are almost ready. Take one out to taste, then turn off the heat once they have your desired chewy texture – be careful not to overcook them, as they will quickly become mushy.

5 Turn off the heat and immediately ladle the hot noodles and broth into serving bowls. Serve with a side of seasoned soy sauce in a small sauce bowl, and black pepper for diners to add to their taste.

KOREAN BBQ: SAMGYEOPSAL, SSAM, SSAMJANG

SIZZLING PORK BELLY

Get ready for a truly special and unforgettable culinary adventure with Korean BBQ, where you're not just eating incredibly tasty food, you're experiencing a vibrant cultural ritual! This isn't your average barbecue; it's a dynamic, interactive feast sizzling right at your table. From succulent cuts of pork belly (samgyeopsal) to exquisitely marinated beef short ribs (yangnyeom galbi), the variety of meats you can barbecue is pretty endless. Many visitors are fascinated by the sizzling experience of barbecuing your own beautifully presented array of meats at the dining table, followed by the uniquely Korean practice of using scissors to expertly snip the grilled meat into bite-sized pieces! The fun continues with 'ssam' culture – the delightful act of wrapping your grilled meat in crisp lettuce or perilla leaves, then customising each bite with grilled garlic, fresh green chilli slices and a dollop of flavourful savoury, spicy dipping sauce known as ssamjang.

This hands-on approach to feasting, combined with the communal joy of cooking and sharing, makes Korean BBQ a must-try experience that will leave you wanting more!

SERVES 3–4

Samgyeopsal

600 g (1 lb 5 oz) fresh pork belly, sliced 1–1.5 cm (½ in) thick

Grill accompaniments

chopped kimchi

sliced garlic cloves

Ssam ingredients, to serve

lettuce or perilla leaves

sliced fresh mild green chillies

Ssamjang (seasoned bean paste, page 194), for dipping

1 Before cooking the pork for the samgyeopsal, have your ssam ingredients set out on the table, ready for serving.

2 If you have a portable gas stove you can set it up on your dining table to cook it tableside, which is how it is traditionally done in Korea. Place your grill pan or skillet over medium-high heat. You won't need to use any cooking oil to cook the samgyeopsal, as the pork will release its own fat.

3 Place the pork belly slices on the hot pan. Cook for 3–5 minutes per side, until beautifully and evenly golden brown and crispy. As it cooks, use kitchen scissors to snip the larger pieces into bite-sized chunks directly on the pan, and add the kimchi and garlic slices to the side of the hot pan to grill alongside the meat.

4 Once cooked, allow diners to assemble their own ssam, wrapping the freshly grilled pork belly in crisp lettuce or perilla leaves with the grilled garlic, fresh green chilli and a dollop of ssamjang – and then enjoying the entire ssam in one bite!

paldo
수정과

KOREAN BBQ

BANCHAN AND SAUCES

Korean BBQ has become popular around the world. These are the essential sauces, banchan and accompaniments to accompany your next KBBQ experience.

Classic BBQ accompaniments and banchan

- Basic wraps and greens (ssam, see page 128): fresh vegetables like lettuce and perilla leaves.
- Fresh garlic and green chilli peppers: often served raw or grilled.
- Kimchi (pages 166, 170 and 172): Kimchi is served both fresh and grilled and can be eaten inside the ssam or as a dish in its own right.
- Pajeori: julienned spring onions (scallions) served in a sesame-chilli dressing, this is especially delicious with barbecued pork belly.
- Yachae jangajji (pickled vegetables, page 176): help to cut the richness of the meat.
- Warm side dishes: there are a number of more substantial side dishes that are typically served alongside Korean BBQ, such as Gyeranjjim (steamed egg custard, page 133), or any jjigae (stew, see pages 78, 81, 82 and 148).
- Ways to finish the meal: a bowl of Mul naengmyeon (cold buckwheat noodle soup, page 69) is a common way to end the meal on a refreshing note.

Dipping sauces for Korean BBQ

- Gireumjang: very simple but essential sauce, particularly for unmarinated meats like pork belly (samgyeopsal) or beef cuts. Made by mixing just three ingredients: sesame oil, salt and ground black pepper.
- Sweet soy dipping sauce: made with soy sauce, vinegar, sugar and water for dipping galbi (ribs) to balance the rich, fatty flavour of the meat and add a clean, refreshing taste.
- Ssamjang (seasoned bean paste, page 194)
- Good quality salt: a must, especially when grilling premium cuts of beef.

수제 꼬치 전문점
족발 보쌈
鷄小舍
제주애월 딱새우

GYERANJJIM

STEAMED EGG CUSTARD

A comforting and universally loved addition to any meal for its cloud-like fluffiness, this savoury steamed egg custard is especially popular to eat alongside a Korean BBQ spread, as its gentle texture and mild flavour perfectly soothe the palate after spicy meats.

SERVES 2 AS A SIDE DISH

- 4 large eggs
- ½ teaspoon fine sea salt
- ¼ teaspoon white sugar
- 1 teaspoon sesame oil
- 1 tablespoon chopped spring onion (scallion)

1 Crack the eggs into a measuring cup or bowl. Add the salt and sugar. Whisk well until the eggs are completely smooth and evenly combined.

2 Place a small earthenware pot on the stove. Add 100 ml (3½ fl oz) water and the sesame oil to the pot and bring to the boil over medium heat.

3 As soon as the water is at a rolling boil, slowly pour the whisked egg mixture into the pot. Immediately use a spatula or spoon to continuously stir the egg mixture in one direction, scraping the bottom of the pot to prevent sticking. Continue stirring until about 70 per cent of the egg mixture has started to set and become visibly lumpy and curdled.

4 At this point, reduce the heat to very low. Cover the pot with a small deep bowl as a lid that allows room for the egg to rise. Leave to steam gently for about 2 minutes. The low heat and steaming action will allow the custard to puff up and cook through without burning the bottom.

5 Carefully remove the lid; your eggs should be beautifully puffed and custardy. Garnish with the spring onion and serve immediately as a warm side dish.

JOKBAL

BRAISED PIG'S TROTTERS

Get ready to discover jokbal, Korea's incredibly popular dish of tender, succulent braised pig's trotters – a true delicacy often enjoyed as a late-night feast! While its savoury, melt-in-your-mouth texture is reason enough to try it, what truly fascinates many is its legendary health benefits: jokbal is famously rich in collagen, great for glowing skin.

The undisputed birthplace of this beloved dish is Jangchung-dong Jokbal Alley in Seoul – a vibrant neighbourhood famed for its specialised jokbal restaurants, each boasting their own secret recipes for long-simmered broths that transform the trotters into a remarkably tender and flavourful experience. Eating jokbal isn't just a meal; it's a dive into Seoul's lively culinary history, a chance to enjoy a gathering with friends, and perhaps, even, a secret to youthful skin!

Rather than rice, jokbal is generally served with a variety of fresh, tangy and savoury accompaniments that balance its rich, fatty flavour. The most common way to enjoy jokbal is by making a ssam – wrapping it in fresh crisp lettuce or perilla leaves with Ssamjang (seasoned bean paste, page 194), sliced raw garlic and/or green chilli for a sharp spicy kick – and eating it in one bite. The salty, briny saeujeot dipping sauce (opposite) is a classic pairing that complements the gelatinous meat incredibly well.

SERVES 6

2 pig's trotters (see Note)

For blanching

- 125 ml (½ cup) soju (Korean distilled spirit) or white wine
- 5 whole garlic cloves, peeled
- 5 bay leaves
- 1 small piece fresh ginger, peeled
- 1 tablespoon whole black peppercorns

Braising broth

- 600 ml (20½ fl oz) jin ganjang (Korean soy sauce)
- 300 ml (10 fl oz) corn syrup (mulyeot)
- 150 ml (5 fl oz) mirim (Korean cooking rice wine)
- 150 ml (5 fl oz) Chinese dark soy sauce
- 300 g (10½ oz) dark brown sugar
- 2 tablespoons doenjang (Korean soybean paste)
- 1 cup whole garlic cloves, peeled
- 1 white onion, peeled and quartered
- 1 apple, cut in half or quartered
- 1 large spring onion (scallion)
- 30 g (1 oz) fresh ginger, peeled and sliced
- 5 star anise
- 1 cinnamon stick
- 1 tablespoon whole black peppercorns

Saeujeot dipping sauce

- 1 tablespoon saeujeot (salted fermented shrimp)
- 1 tablespoon sesame oil
- 1 teaspoon gochugaru (Korean chilli flakes)
- 1 teaspoon toasted sesame seeds
- 1 green chilli, finely chopped
- 2 tablespoons water

1 Soak the trotters in cold water for a minimum of 3 hours to thoroughly remove the blood, as blood trapped in the bones is a primary source of gamey odour. Press firmly on the trotters with gloved hands periodically to help release the blood, and change the water every hour or so.

2 Drain the trotters, then place in a large saucepan, cover with fresh water and bring to the boil. Add all the blanching ingredients and return to a rolling boil, then continue to boil for another 5 minutes. This blanching step helps to clean the trotters and remove any remaining impurities. Drain the trotters again and rinse thoroughly under cold running water.

3 Use a kitchen blow torch to carefully singe off any remaining fine hairs on the trotters, to ensure the skin has a clean and smooth texture.

4 Place all the braising broth ingredients in a large stockpot. Pour in 3 litres (3 quarts) water and bring to the boil. Add the cleaned trotters, then reduce the heat to medium and cover. (The lid traps steam and moisture inside the pot, which helps the tough connective tissue break down and become succulent.) Simmer for 1½ hours, ensuring the trotters remain fully submerged.

5 Before removing from the heat, turn off the stove and let the trotters 'rest' in the hot broth for a further 10 minutes. This resting period allows the meat to become even more tender and absorb more flavour.

6 Carefully transfer the trotters to a rack set over a tray. Cover loosely with plastic wrap and let them cool for 30 minutes. It's crucial to cool the trotters before slicing, otherwise the meat and skin may separate, affecting the final texture and presentation.

7 Meanwhile, combine all the dipping sauce ingredients in a small bowl, mixing well.

8 Once the trotters have cooled, use a sharp knife to carefully separate the meat from the bone, keeping the skin intact, and cutting close to the bone in a circular motion. Thinly slice the meat.

9 Serve immediately, with the dipping sauce.

Note

Ask your butcher for the front trotters, rather than the hind trotters. The front trotters are much meatier and have a higher ratio of skin, fat and gelatinous tissue, making them tastier.

BOSSAM

WRAPPED PORK WITH RADISH KIMCHI

Bossam literally means 'wrapped', and that's exactly how you eat this truly delightful Korean dish centred around tender, succulent slices of boiled pork – by creating a perfect, flavourful parcel of pork belly, kimchi and chilli!

Unlike other pork dishes, bossam is all about the pure, rich taste of the pork, which is simmered until incredibly tender. You then take a piece of this delicious meat and wrap it in fresh lettuce or perilla leaves, adding your favourite condiments. The most essential companion is fresh, crispy mu-kimchi (radish kimchi) or a spicy radish salad, the clean crunch and vibrant kick perfectly complementing the savoury pork.

Bossam holds a particularly special place in Korean culture on Kimjang Day – a huge annual event where families and communities gather to make large batches of kimchi to sustain them through the winter months. After hours of hard work, there's no better reward than sitting down together to enjoy freshly made, still-warm bossam with the very first batches of the season's new kimchi. It's a heartwarming tradition that embodies community, delicious food and the deep satisfaction of shared effort.

SERVES 4

- 1.2 kg (2 lb 10 oz) pork belly
- 2 large spring onions (scallions), cut into 10 cm (4 in) lengths
- 1 onion, sliced 2 cm (¾ in) thick
- 10 whole garlic cloves, peeled
- 30 g (1 oz) fresh ginger, peeled and sliced
- 5 bay leaves
- 1 tablespoon whole black peppercorns
- 125 ml (½ cup) mirim (Korean rice cooking wine)
- 2 tablespoons doenjang (Korean soybean paste)

1 Pat the pork belly thoroughly dry with paper towel to remove any excess blood.

2 Place the spring onion pieces and onion wedges in a large saucepan, to create a bed. Place the pork on top. Add the garlic cloves, ginger slices, bay leaves, peppercorns, mirim and doenjang to the pan, directly over and around the pork.

3 Pour enough water into the pan to fully submerge the pork. Cover and bring to the boil over medium-high heat.

4 Once boiling, reduce the heat to medium and continue to simmer for about 50 minutes. To check if the pork is cooked through, pierce it with a paring knife or a chopstick; if clear juices run out and there's no pink, it's done. The actual cooking time may vary slightly depending on the thickness of the pork and the heat of your stove.

5 Once tender, transfer the pork to a cutting board. Let it cool slightly for a few minutes to allow the juices to redistribute before slicing; this helps prevent the meat and skin separating.

6 Carve the pork belly into slices about 1 cm (½ in) thick. Serve immediately as a shared platter meal, with fresh leafy greens for diners to wrap and assemble their own bossam, with the green chilli slices, ssamjang dipping sauce and the mu-kimchi on the side.

Mu-kimchi (radish kimchi)

- 600 g (1 lb 5 oz) Korean radish (use the greener, sweeter bottom part of the radish)
- 1 tablespoon coarse sea salt
- 80 ml (⅓ cup) corn syrup (mulyeot)
- 3 tablespoons gochugaru (Korean chilli flakes)
- 2 tablespoons anchovy fish sauce (myeolchi aekjeot)
- 2 teaspoons minced garlic

Ssam ingredients, to serve

- lettuce or perilla leaves
- sliced fresh mild green chillies
- Ssamjang (seasoned bean paste, page 194), for dipping
- Saeujeot dipping sauce (page 135)

Mu-kimchi

1 Peel the radish, then slice into rounds about 2 mm (1/16 in) thick. Then julienne these rounds into 3 mm (1/10 in) thick strips.

2 Place the julienned radish in a bowl. Add the coarse sea salt and corn syrup and mix well to combine. Let the radish sit for 30 minutes to draw out its moisture; after this time, you'll see a good amount of liquid released from the radish.

3 Transfer the radish to a colander, then firmly squeeze the radish with both hands to extract as much excess water as possible. This step is key for achieving that desirable crunchy texture.

4 Put the squeezed radish into a clean bowl. Add the gochugaru and mix thoroughly until the radish is evenly coated. Adding the gochugaru at this stage helps absorb any residual surface moisture and ensures a vibrant, beautiful colour.

5 Add the remaining kimchi ingredients. Using your hands, thoroughly mix and massage the radish and seasonings until everything is well combined and evenly coated. Taste and adjust the seasoning if needed. Mu-kimchi is typically enjoyed when it is fresh and crunchy. For the best flavour and texture, keep in an airtight container in the fridge and use within a day or two of making.

GALBI-JJIM

BRAISED BEEF SHORT RIBS

Historically, galbi-jjim was a royal dish, once gracing the King's table in the Joseon dynasty. These days, these exquisitely tender, fall-off-the-bone beef short ribs are a celebrated centrepiece of Korean festive tables for holidays and family celebrations, being a dish that still deeply embodies prosperity and abundance. To taste galbi-jjim is to taste a piece of Korean culinary heritage - a luxurious and universally loved dish that continues to bring families together.

SERVES 4

- 2 kg (2 lb 10 oz) beef short ribs for stewing
- 1 tablespoon white sugar
- 125 ml (½ cup) soju (Korean distilled spirit) or white wine
- 4 bay leaves
- 1 tablespoon whole black peppercorns
- ⅓ Korean radish
- ½ carrot
- 4 fresh shiitake mushrooms
- 2 large spring onions (scallions), white part only, sliced diagonally into 2 cm (¾ in) pieces

Marinade

- 1 Korean pear (or 1 sweet apple), peeled
- 4 tablespoons white sugar
- 4 tablespoons minced garlic
- 3 tablespoons finely chopped spring onion (scallion), white part only
- 1 tablespoon minced ginger
- 200 ml (7 fl oz) jin ganjang (Korean soy sauce)
- 80 ml (⅓ cup) oligo syrup
- 2 tablespoons sesame oil
- 30 ml (1 fl oz) mirim (Korean cooking rice wine)
- ½ teaspoon ground black pepper
- 600 ml (20½ fl oz) water

1 Rinse the ribs under cold running water. Place them in a large bowl and cover completely with cold water. Add the sugar to the soaking water; this helps draw out the blood more effectively. Let the ribs soak for 2 hours, changing the water once or twice to ensure a cleaner broth.

2 Drain the ribs, place in a large saucepan and cover with plenty of fresh water. Add the soju, bay leaves and peppercorns. Bring to a rolling boil over medium-high heat, then leave to boil for about 15 minutes, stirring occasionally to ensure even blanching. This step removes impurities, any gamey odour, and helps tenderise the meat, leading to a much cleaner and smoother final stew.

3 Drain the ribs in a colander. Rinse each rib thoroughly under cold running water, scrubbing gently with your hands to remove any impurities, bone fragments or solidified fat that may be clinging to the bones. Clean out the pan as well.

4 Cut the radish and carrot into 3 cm (1¼ in) thick slices, then quarter them. Use a peeler to round off the sharp edges of the radish and carrot pieces for a more appealing presentation, and to prevent them breaking apart during simmering.

5 Place the radish in a large, deep saucepan, then arrange the blanched ribs on top.

6 To make the marinade, place the pear and spring onion in a blender and process until fully pureed and very smooth, to help tenderise the meat. Transfer to a large bowl, then add the remaining marinade ingredients and mix until well combined. (Avoid blending all the marinade ingredients together in the blender as this can create too much foam and alter the texture.)

7 Pour the marinade evenly over the ribs. Cover and bring to the boil over medium-high heat, then reduce the heat to medium-low and let it simmer for 40–45 minutes, until the ribs are about halfway tender.

8 Score the tops of the shiitake mushrooms with a cross shape. Add them to the pan with the carrot, then cover and simmer for a further 15 minutes, or until the ribs are very tender.

9 Finally, add the spring onion and simmer for another 5–10 minutes, until the spring onion is soft.

10 Serve hot, with warm rice (see pages 186 or 188).

GAMJATANG

SPICY PORK BACK-BONE STEW

While its exact origin is debated, some believe this famously hearty and spicy pork back-bone soup began with labourers who needed a cheap yet nutritious meal. Gamjatang is a robust and deeply satisfying dish guaranteed to warm your soul, and it pairs perfectly with a shot of soju (a Korean distilled spirit).

SERVES 4

- 1 kg (2 lb 3 oz) pork neck bones or back bones
- 1 tablespoon white sugar
- 350 g (12½ oz) wombok (Chinese cabbage)
- 400 g (14 oz) potatoes, peeled and halved or quartered, depending on size
- 100 g (3½ oz) large spring onions (scallions), sliced diagonally
- 35 g (1 cup) perilla leaves (if unavailable, simply omit)
- 80 g (2¾ oz) roasted perilla seed powder (see Note)

Broth

- 125 ml (½ cup) mirim (Korean cooking rice wine)
- 30 g (1 oz) fresh ginger, peeled
- ½ onion, roughly chopped
- 3 bay leaves
- 1 teaspoon whole black peppercorns

1 Place the pork bones in a large bowl, then cover with enough cold water to fully submerge the bones. Add the sugar to the water and let the bones soak for about 1 hour to thoroughly remove the blood, which is key for reducing gamey odours.

2 Drain the soaked bones, then place them in a large saucepan. Add the broth ingredients and 2 litres (2 quarts) water. Bring to a rolling boil over high heat, then reduce the heat to medium and leave to simmer for 1 hour. This process helps tenderise the meat and remove any remaining impurities and strong odours.

3 Carefully remove the pork bones from the pan. Strain the broth through a fine-mesh sieve into a clean bowl, discarding all the solids and aromatics. Set the broth aside.

4 Rinse each pork bone thoroughly under cold running water, scrubbing gently to remove any clinging impurities or solidified fat.

5 Trim away the core end of the cabbage then separate the leaves. Gently blanch the leaves in a saucepan of boiling water for about 1 minute, until slightly softened. Immediately transfer to cold water to cool, then squeeze out the excess water.

6 In a large bowl, combine the seasoning paste ingredients, mixing well until a thick, smooth paste forms. Add the blanched cabbage to the seasoning paste and mix thoroughly.

Seasoning paste

- 80 ml (⅓ cup) mirim (Korean cooking rice wine)
- 4 tablespoons gochugaru (Korean chilli flakes)
- 2 tablespoons doenjang (Korean soybean paste)
- 2 tablespoons tuna extract (chamchi-aek)
- 1 tablespoon guk ganjang (Korean soup soy sauce)
- 3 tablespoons minced garlic
- 1 tablespoon minced ginger
- 1 tablespoon white sugar
- ½ teaspoon ground black pepper

Note
Made from roasted and ground perilla seeds, and known in Korean as deulkkae-garu, roasted perilla seed powder is a key ingredient that gives gamjatang its signature deep savoury flavour. It has a wonderfully rich and earthy taste. It also acts as a natural thickener, giving the stew a hearty, velvety consistency. It is sold in most Korean or Asian grocery stores, usually in bags or tubs in the seasoning aisle.

7 Place the cleaned pork bones in a large clean saucepan. Pour in 1.5 litres (6 cups) of the pork broth. Add the marinated cabbage and the potatoes. Bring to a strong boil over high heat, then reduce the heat to medium–low and let the stew simmer for an additional 30 minutes.

8 Finally, add the spring onion, perilla leaves and perilla seed powder and stir gently to combine. Simmer for another 2–3 minutes to allow these last aromatics to infuse into the stew.

9 Serve hot, preferably in a warm earthenware pot, with rice (see pages 186 or 188) and kimchi. Other perfect accompaniments are Kkakdugi (diced radish kimchi, page 172), Samsaek namul (seasoned vegetables, page 40), Gyeran-mari (rolled omelette, page 26) and Gim gui (toasted seaweed sheets, page 178) – their simple or refreshing taste balances the bold flavours of this stew.

곱창
순대
허파
껍데기

JJIMDAK

SWEET SOY SAUCE BRAISED CHICKEN

Jjimdak is a popular Korean dish from the city of Andong, in the country's east. It is an evolution of a special steamed chicken dish that was traditionally prepared for important guests in a wealthy village during the Joseon dynasty. Designed for sharing, jjimdak is a generous, comforting meal that brings a touch of historical grandeur to your table!

SERVES 4

- 60 g (2 oz) dangmyeon (Korean sweet potato starch noodles)
- 1 whole chicken, cut into 8 pieces
- 2 tablespoons mirim (Korean cooking rice wine)
- 2 teaspoons whole black peppercorns
- 2 dried red chillies, cut in half
- 2 potatoes, quartered into large chunks
- 1 onion, quartered into large chunks
- ½ carrot, quartered into large chunks
- 1 large spring onion (scallion), sliced diagonally into 2 cm (¾ in) pieces
- 1 tablespoon sesame oil
- toasted sesame seeds, for sprinkling

Braising sauce

- 100 ml (3½ fl oz) jin ganjang (Korean soy sauce)
- 90 ml (3 fl oz) mirim (Korean cooking rice wine)
- 50 g (1¾ oz) white sugar
- 1 tablespoon Chinese dark soy sauce
- 1 tablespoon oyster sauce
- 1 tablespoon oligo syrup
- 1 tablespoon minced garlic
- 1 teaspoon minced ginger
- ¼ teaspoon ground black pepper

1 Place the noodles in a rectangular tray (or any container long enough for the noodles to lie flat in). Pour enough cold water to completely submerge them, then let the noodles soak for at least 30 minutes.

2 Meanwhile, place the chicken pieces in a large saucepan and pour in enough water to fully submerge them. Add the mirim and peppercorns and bring the water to a rolling boil. Blanch the chicken for about 5 minutes to remove impurities and any gamey odour.

3 Drain the chicken in a colander. Rinse each chicken piece thoroughly under cold running water, scrubbing gently to remove any remaining scum or impurities.

4 Place the chicken in a large wok or large clean saucepan. In a bowl, whisk together all the braising sauce ingredients until the sugar is fully dissolved, then pour over the chicken, along with 500 ml (2 cups) water.

5 Bring the mixture to a strong boil over high heat, using a ladle to skim off any foam or impurities that rise to the surface. Add the dried chillies, reduce the heat to medium, then cover and leave to simmer for 10 minutes, allowing the chicken to absorb the flavours.

6 Add another 250 ml (1 cup) water, along with the potatoes, onion and carrot. Stir gently, then cover and simmer over medium heat for another 15 minutes, or until the vegetables are tender and the chicken is cooked.

7 Drain the noodles well, then add to the braise with the spring onion. Simmer, uncovered, over medium heat for another 5 minutes, until the noodles become translucent and are fully cooked.

8 Turn off the heat. Drizzle with the sesame oil and sprinkle generously with toasted sesame seeds.

9 Serve immediately with rice (see pages 186 or 188) and kimchi, Yachae jangajji (pickled vegetables, page 176), Oi muchim (cucumber salad, page 175) and light soups.

포차
30
여기부터
일방
꼬막.석화
오돌뼈 제육볶음
수제햄버거
진한 멸치국수
수제 햄버거

POCHA CULTURE

The soul of Korean nightlife.

Beyond the bustling BBQ joints and delivery scooters lies another beloved facet of Korean night culture: the Pocha. Short for pojangmacha, which literally means 'covered wagon', pochas are informal, often tented, street-side eateries or casual indoor establishments that are synonymous with late-night conversations, comfort food and drinks. They offer a raw, authentic glimpse into the lively Korean social scene.

Jongno Pocha Street is the most lively pocha street in Seoul. The atmosphere is unpretentious and incredibly welcoming. You'll find people from all walks of life unwinding after work, friends catching up and couples enjoying casual dates. The sounds of sizzling food, clinking soju glasses and animated chatter fill the air, creating a truly immersive experience. This is where Koreans go to de-stress, share their day's stories and connect.

Pochas specialise in delicious food that's often spicy but always comforting. These dishes are perfect for sharing, especially when accompanied by soju (Korea's ubiquitous distilled spirit) or beer. The food is designed to be flavourful and satisfying, making it the ideal anju (food eaten with alcohol).

While many bunsik (flour-based snacks) like Tteokbokki (stir-fried rice cakes, page 51) and twigim (deep-fried snacks, similar to Japanese tempura) can be found on the menu, pochas often offer a wider range of hearty dishes. Pocha culture is an integral part of experiencing Korean nightlife. It's about the joy of sharing simple, delicious food, drinking with friends and letting loose in an atmosphere that is uniquely Korean.

BUDAE JJIGAE

KOREAN SAUSAGE ARMY STEW

Affectionately known as 'army stew', this bubbling satisfying dish has a fascinating, bittersweet history, emerging from the challenging times following the Korean War. In those lean years, resourceful Koreans near US military bases, particularly in areas like Uijeongbu, began making use of surplus American ingredients such as Spam and hot dogs, and what started out as a simple stew, eaten out of necessity, soon evolved as Koreans ingeniously added their staples such as kimchi, gochujang, tofu and ramen noodles – whatever was available – creating the unique budae jjigae we know today.

This hearty stew speaks of Korean creativity and resilience, transforming hardship into a beloved culinary icon. With its adaptable mix of meats and vegetables, delivered with a spicy kick, budae jjigae is a must-try dish – a truly comforting and flavourful piece of Korean history on your table.

SERVES 4

- 200 g (7 oz) tin Spam
- 4 hot dog sausages
- ½ onion, thinly sliced
- 1 large spring onion (scallion), sliced diagonally
- 150 g (5½ oz) firm tofu
- 50 g (1¾ oz) minced (ground) beef
- 4 tablespoons baked beans
- 2 slices cheddar cheese
- 300 ml (10 fl oz) store-bought beef bone broth (sagol gomtang yuksu), or Anchovy-kelp broth (page 192) for a lighter flavour
- 1 packet instant ramen noodles

Seasoning paste

- 4 tablespoons gochugaru (Korean chilli flakes)
- 2 tablespoons jin ganjang (Korean soy sauce)
- 2 tablespoons mirim (Korean cooking rice wine)
- 2 tablespoons minced garlic
- ¼ teaspoon ground black pepper

1 For a cleaner taste, briefly blanch the Spam and sausages in a saucepan of boiling water for 1–2 minutes, to help remove the excess oil and the processed meat flavour. Drain well.

2 Keeping the original block shape, cut the Spam into slices about 5 mm (¼ in) thick, and cut the sausages into long diagonal slices about 5 mm (¼ in) thick.

3 Combine all the seasoning paste ingredients in a small bowl, mixing well until a smooth paste forms.

4 Spread the onion and spring onion slices in the bottom of a wide, shallow hot pot or saucepan.

5 Slice the tofu block in half lengthways, then cut into 1 cm (½ in) thick slices.

6 Neatly arrange the Spam, sausages and tofu around the pot. Place the raw beef in the centre, then dollop the seasoning paste on top of the beef.

7 Spoon the baked beans next to the seasoning paste and place the two cheese slices either on top of the seasoning or on each side.

8 Pour the broth and 300 ml (10 fl oz) water into the pot and place over high heat. Once the broth starts to boil, reduce the heat to medium. Gently stir the seasoning paste into the broth until it dissolves, then leave to simmer for about 10 minutes.

9 Once the beef is cooked through, add the instant noodles (but not the contents of the ready-made noodle seasoning packet). Continue to boil for about 3 minutes, or until the noodles are cooked to your preference.

10 Serve immediately.

DAKBOK-KEUMTANG

SPICY BRAISED CHICKEN

Packed with tender chicken, potatoes and vegetables braised in a robust, flavourful gochujang-based sauce, this family favourite is perfect for a cosy meal – warming and incredibly satisfying, with a delicious balance of spice and richness.

SERVES 4

- 1 whole chicken, about 1.2 kg (2 lb 10 oz), cut into 8 pieces
- 2 tablespoons mirim (Korean cooking rice wine)
- 2 potatoes, cut into 2 cm (¾ in) chunks
- 1 onion, cut into large wedges
- ½ carrot, cut into large chunks
- 1 large spring onion (scallion), sliced diagonally

Seasoning sauce

- 4 tablespoons gochujang (Korean chilli paste)
- 80 ml (⅓ cup) jin ganjang (Korean soy sauce)
- 2 tablespoons gochugaru (Korean chilli flakes)
- 2 tablespoons white sugar
- 1 tablespoon minced garlic
- ¼ teaspoon ground black pepper
- 600 ml (20½ fl oz) water

1 Rinse the chicken pieces thoroughly under cold running water. Bring a large saucepan of water to a rolling boil. Add the chicken pieces and mirim. Blanch the chicken for about 5 minutes to remove impurities and any gamey odour. Drain the chicken in a colander and rinse each piece again under cold running water to remove any remaining scum.

2 In a bowl, combine all the seasoning sauce ingredients. Mix well until the gochujang and sugar are fully dissolved, creating a smooth sauce.

3 Place the blanched chicken pieces in a wok or large saucepan. Pour the seasoning sauce over the chicken. Bring to the boil over high heat, then reduce the heat to medium. Cover and simmer for 20 minutes, stirring occasionally to ensure even cooking and prevent sticking.

4 Add the potato, onion and carrot. Cover and simmer over medium heat for another 15 minutes, or until the vegetables are tender and the sauce has thickened slightly, stirring occasionally to ensure all ingredients are well coated and cooked through.

5 Finally, add the spring onion and cook for another 2–3 minutes, until softened slightly.

6 Serve hot, with rice (see pages 186 or 188); it also pairs well with kimchi and simple vegetable side dishes like Kong namul (seasoned bean sprouts, page 40) or tangy Oi muchim (cucumber salad, page 175).

조개모듬탕구이
NEW YORK
국산여수골뱅이
빨낙지
국산 뻘낙지
살아있는 뻘낙지
새우1kg

HAEMUL JJIM

SPICY BRAISED SEAFOOD

Packed with a generous medley of fresh seafood including octopus, crab and shellfish, all tossed in a fiery, garlicky sauce, haemul jjim is a bold, spicy, vibrant feast of a dish that truly awakens the senses and showcases Korea's love for seafood.

SERVES 4

300 g (10½ oz) king tiger prawns (shrimp)

1 crab, 300–400 g (10½–14 oz) total weight

200 g (7 oz) octopus or squid

200 g (7 oz) large scallops

200 g (7 oz) firm white fish fillets, such as cod or snapper

1 tablespoon vegetable oil

600 g (1 lb 5 oz) mung bean sprouts

60 ml (¼ cup) mirim (Korean cooking rice wine)

2 tablespoons potato starch, mixed to a smooth slurry with 80 ml (⅓ cup) water

½ white onion, sliced lengthways about 1 cm (½ in) thick

1 large spring onion (scallion), sliced diagonally

1 tablespoon sesame oil

toasted sesame seeds, for sprinkling

Spicy sauce

3 tablespoons minced garlic

1 teaspoon minced ginger

50–60 g (1¾–2 oz) gochugaru (Korean chilli flakes)

2 tablespoons tuna extract (chamchi-aek)

2 tablespoons mirim (Korean cooking rice wine)

2 tablespoons oligo syrup

1 tablespoon jin ganjang (Korean soy sauce)

¼ teaspoon ground black pepper

1 Peel and devein the prawns, removing the heads.

2 Clean the crab, removing the gills and spongy parts, and chop into two to four pieces, depending on its size.

3 Clean the squid thoroughly by removing the internal organs and the clear cartilage from inside the body, as well as the beak and eyes. Cut the body into 2.5 cm (1 in) slices and the tentacles into 5–7.5 cm (2–3 in) lengths (they will shrink considerably when cooked).

4 Clean the scallops and cut away the small, tough muscle on the side.

5 Check the fish fillets for any fine bones and remove them (you can leave the skin on). Rinse the fillets, pat dry and cut into 2.5 cm (1 in) chunks.

6 In a bowl, whisk together all the spicy sauce ingredients until well combined.

7 Drizzle the vegetable oil into a large wok. Arrange all the seafood evenly on the bottom of the wok, then cover with the bean sprouts. Pour the mirim over the bean sprouts. Cover with a lid and steam over high heat for about 5 minutes; this step helps to reduce any fishy odours and par-cooks the bean sprouts.

8 Remove the lid; you will notice liquid released from the bean sprouts and seafood. Add the onion and spring onion and drizzle the spicy sauce all over the top. Increase the heat to high and stir-fry everything well to thoroughly mix the sauce through.

9 After 5–7 minutes, once the seafood is almost cooked and the sauce is bubbling, slowly add the potato starch slurry in two or three batches, stirring constantly, and adding just enough to reach your desired consistency; the sauce should be thick enough to cling to the seafood and vegetables.

10 Turn off the heat. Drizzle with the sesame oil and sprinkle generously with toasted sesame seeds. Serve immediately, with warm rice (see pages 186 or 188).

OJINGEO BOKKEUM

STIR-FRIED SPICY SQUID

Ignite your taste buds with one of Korea's favourite fiery stir-fried seafood dishes! Historically, squid has been abundant and affordable, especially in the East Sea, making dishes such as ojingeo bokkeum accessible and deliciously convenient staples for home kitchens – as well as being commonly served in restaurants.

Ojingeo bokkeum is spicy, savoury and slightly sweet – making it a perfect rice thief (something so delicious you end up eating a lot of rice with it).

SERVES 2

- 200 g (7 oz) squid (or octopus)
- 2 tablespoons vegetable oil
- ⅓ large spring onion (scallion), diagonally sliced
- ½ onion, thinly sliced
- ⅓ carrot, thinly sliced or julienned
- 1–2 green chillies, thinly sliced
- 1 teaspoon sesame oil
- sesame seeds, for sprinkling

Seasoning sauce

- 1 tablespoon gochugaru (Korean chilli flakes)
- 1 tablespoon gochujang (Korean chilli paste)
- 1 tablespoon jin ganjang (Korean soy sauce)
- 1 tablespoon mirim (Korean cooking rice wine)
- 1 tablespoon white sugar
- 1 teaspoon minced garlic

1 Clean the squid thoroughly by removing the internal organs and the clear cartilage from inside the body, as well as the beak and eyes. Use a paper towel to help rub off the thin outer skin from the body. Prepare the tentacles by cutting them off the head, then cutting the entire cluster into two or three pieces. Slice the squid body into 1 cm (½ in) rings.

2 In a small bowl, mix together all the seasoning sauce ingredients until the sugar is fully dissolved and everything is well combined.

3 Heat a large non-stick wok or frying pan over medium heat. Add the vegetable oil. Once hot, add the spring onion and stir-fry for about 1 minute, until fragrant and lightly browned, to infuse the oil.

4 Add the squid, onion, carrot and chilli and stir-fry rapidly over high heat for 1 minute. Pour the seasoning sauce over and stir-fry for a further 1 minute, ensuring the squid is coated in the sauce.

5 Reduce the heat to medium-low. Cover with a lid and let the squid steam for 2 minutes. This allows the squid to release its natural moisture and become tender without overcooking.

6 Turn off the heat. Drizzle with the sesame oil, sprinkle with toasted sesame seeds and toss everything together one last time.

7 Serve immediately, with warm rice (see pages 186 or 188), kimchi and Gyeranjjim (steamed egg custard, page 133) to gently soothe the spiciness, or Samsaek namul (seasoned vegetables, page 40) for some freshness.

홀덤
이벤트 펍
구월점
446-1119
6F
CUBE
큐브노래타운
인쌩맥주
궁
노래
타운
삼겹살
백반정식
웰빙
삼순이
삼겹살
백반정식
TERRA
루프
나인
PC
CAFE
7F
쥬얼리
6층

SOSIJI YACHAE BOKKEUM

STIR-FRIED SAUSAGE WITH VEGETABLES

A versatile crowd-pleaser that perfectly blends convenience with comforting flavours. This simple yet satisfying stir-fry features colourful vegetables and sausages, and is a popular anju (drinking snack) for adults, but is equally loved as a fun and convenient side dish for kids.

SERVES 2 AS A SIDE DISH

200 g (7 oz) small hot dog sausages

vegetable oil, for stir-frying

½ white onion, cut into 2 cm (¾ in) cubes

⅓ carrot, cut into 5 mm (¼ in) thick half-moons

⅓ red bell pepper (capsicum), cut into 2 cm (¾ in) cubes

⅓ yellow bell pepper (capsicum), cut into 2 cm (¾ in) cubes

Stir-fry sauce

3 tablespoons tomato ketchup

1 tablespoon gochujang (Korean chilli paste)

1 tablespoon oligo syrup

1 tablespoon white sugar

2 teaspoons jin ganjang (Korean soy sauce)

1 teaspoon oyster sauce

1 tablespoon water

1 To prepare the sausages, make small diagonal incisions about halfway through each sausage. Space the incisions 0.5 cm (⅕ in) apart so that each sausage has 3–4 incisions.

2 In a small bowl, combine all the stir-fry sauce ingredients, mixing well until smoothly combined.

3 Heat 1–2 tablespoons vegetable oil in a frying pan over medium heat. Add the scored sausages, onion and carrot. Cook for 1–2 minutes, stirring occasionally, until the scored parts of the sausages begin to slightly open up.

4 Add the bell peppers and stir-fry for about 3 minutes, ensuring the vegetables remain slightly crisp and don't become too soft or mushy.

5 Pour the stir-fry sauce into the pan. Stir-fry for another 2–3 minutes, coating all the ingredients evenly with the sauce, until the sauce thickens slightly and clings to the sausages and vegetables.

6 Serve immediately as a delicious side dish with warm freshly cooked rice (see pages 186 or 188).

SIKHYE

SWEET RICE PUNCH

Step into Korea's festive traditions with sikhye, a beloved non-alcoholic beverage enjoyed during holidays such as Seollal (Korean Lunar New Year). Generally served cold, and often featuring a few floating rice grains, sikhye offers a unique, refreshing sweetness with a hint of malt. For an invigorating contrast, try the spiced cinnamon punch known as sujeonggwa on page 160. Both offer a delightful taste of traditional Korean celebrations.

Sikhye is a great dessert drink to enjoy after dinner. Its refreshing sweetness serves as a perfect palate cleanser, and the malted barley is known to aid digestion, making it a soothing way to finish a meal.

MAKES 3 LITRES (3 QUARTS)

- 220 g (1 cup) short-grain white rice
- 300 g (10½ oz) malted barley powder (yeot-gireum)
- 160 g (5½ oz) white sugar
- 1 small piece fresh ginger (approx. 1-2 cm/½–¾ in), peeled

1 Place the rice in a saucepan with 250 ml (1 cup) water. Bring to the boil over high heat, then immediately reduce the heat to low, cover the pan and simmer for 10–12 minutes. Turn off the heat and let the rice steam, still covered, for a further 10 minutes. The rice should be cooked through, but with individual firm grains that are not clumped together. It's important that the rice grains are not soft or sticky, as this helps them separate during the fermentation process. Set aside to cool down while proceeding with the recipe.

2 Place the barley powder in a fine-mesh cloth bag. Tie the bag securely, then place in a deep pot or large bowl. Pour 1.5 litres (6 cups) warm water over the bag and let it soak for 1 hour.

3 Using both hands, firmly squeeze and knead the malted barley bag over the same bowl, to catch all the milky white liquid that is being extracted. Continue kneading thoroughly until no more milky liquid is released, reserving the milky liquid.

4 Place the barley bag back in the same pot or bowl. Add another 1.5 litres (6 cups) warm water. Firmly squeeze and knead the bag again to extract more liquid. Discard the barley bag, but let the extracted milky barley liquid sit for about 30 minutes. This allows the sediment (starch residue) to settle at the bottom.

5 Place the cooked rice in the bottom of a deep oven-safe container. Carefully pour only the clear top layer of the settled barley liquid into the container, leaving the thick sediment behind. Add 2 tablespoons of the sugar.

6 Set your oven to 50–60°C (122–140°F) and leave the rice in the oven to ferment for 5–6 hours.

7 After 5 hours, check if some rice grains (around 20) have floated to the surface. If so, the mixture is well fermented. If not, continue fermenting a bit longer.

8 Carefully transfer the fermented liquid (including the rice grains) to a large saucepan.

9 Add the remaining sugar and the ginger. Bring to the boil over medium heat, then simmer for about 15 minutes, continually skimming off any white foam that rises to the surface.

10 Remove the ginger and leave to cool completely to room temperature.

11 Transfer the punch to a large clean pitcher or several bottles and chill in the fridge. Sikhye is best served cold, especially after rich or spicy meals.

Note

Your sikhye will keep well in the fridge for several days. For longer storage, it can be frozen for several months. The cold temperature of the fridge significantly slows down the fermentation process, but doesn't stop it completely. Over time, the flavour will change as the fermentation continues very slowly. If left beyond about 5 days, the punch will start to taste more sour, and may eventually spoil. It's best consumed within the first few days for the freshest and most balanced flavour.

SUJEONGGWA

CINNAMON PUNCH

This traditional cinnamon punch is often enjoyed during holidays in Korea. The dried persimmons are added to the punch after the spices have steeped and the liquid has cooled, allowing them to soften naturally and impart a gentle sweetness and subtly spicy flavour without losing their shape. Although the punch is served chilled, it is nevertheless a warming, refreshing and invigorating drink that provides a delightful contrast to richer festive foods, leaving a clean, comforting finish at the end of a meal.

MAKES ABOUT 2 LITRES (2 QUARTS)

- 100 g (3½ oz) fresh ginger
- 90 g (3 oz) whole cinnamon sticks
- 150 g (5½ oz) dark brown sugar
- 5 dried persimmons, deseeded and cut into small pieces
- pine nuts, to garnish
- 1 tablespoon water

1 Thoroughly wash the ginger. Use a spoon to scrape off the skin, then cut the ginger into slices about 3 mm (1/10 in) thick.

2 Break the whole cinnamon sticks in half. Use a clean brush with soft bristles (such as a pastry brush) to remove any dust or impurities from the inner and outer surfaces, or just rinse them thoroughly.

3 Pour 2 litres (2 quarts) water into a large saucepan. Add the ginger slices and cinnamon sticks and bring to a rolling boil over high heat. Once boiling, reduce the heat to medium-low and leave to simmer gently for 1 hour, to extract the maximum flavour from the spices.

4 Line a fine-mesh sieve with muslin (cheesecloth) and place over a clean saucepan. Carefully pour the liquid through the sieve and into the pan, straining out all the spices, leaving only a clear, aromatic liquid.

5 Add the sugar to the strained liquid. Bring back to the boil over high heat, then leave to boil for another 10 minutes, stirring occasionally to ensure the sugar fully dissolves.

6 Remove from the heat and allow to cool down to room temperature.

7 Once cooled, add the dried persimmon and transfer the punch to a large clean airtight container or several bottles.

8 Refrigerate for at least 2 days or up to 3 days, to allow the flavours to deepen and mature. This steeping period is essential for the best taste.

9 When ready to serve, pour the chilled punch into small glasses. Float a few pine nuts on top of each glass as a garnish and enjoy!

BASICS

FERMENTED FOODS

The secret to Korean flavour.

At the very heart of Korean cuisine lies a profound appreciation for fermented foods. These culinary powerhouses are not just ingredients; they are the soul of countless dishes, imbuing them with unique, deep flavours and offering remarkable health benefits. For Koreans, fermentation is an ancient art that transforms simple ingredients into complex and indispensable staples of daily life.

To truly understand Korean flavours, you must be acquainted with what we affectionately call the 'holy trinity' of Korean cuisine, gochujang, doenjang and ganjang – the three core fermented pastes and sauces that form the backbone of almost every Korean pantry. Crucially, all of these ingredients begin their journey with meju, a block of fermented soybeans. This foundational ingredient is what gives each of these ingredients their unique depth and character.

Gochujang

This vibrant red paste is made from gochugaru (Korean chilli flakes), glutinous rice and salt, all combined with fermented soybean powder (which has been derived from meju). Its flavour profile is incredibly complex: simultaneously sweet and spicy with a delightful umami depth. Gochujang is incredibly versatile and is a key part of iconic dishes like Tteokbokki (stir-fried rice cakes, page 51), Bibimbap (mixed rice with vegetables, page 62), and various spicy stews and marinades, including Jeyukbokkeum (stir-fried spicy pork, page 52). It adds not just heat, but a rich, nuanced flavour that simply can't be replicated.

Doenjang

Doenjang is a rich, savoury paste made directly from fermented soybeans (meju) and salt. Unlike Japanese miso, Korean doenjang often has a coarser texture and a much earthier and more robust flavour profile, sometimes with nutty undertones. It has a pungent aroma which mellows beautifully when cooked. Doenjang is the base for Doenjang jjigae (soybean paste stew, page 78), a staple of the Korean table. It's also used in marinades, dipping sauces and as a key seasoning for various vegetable dishes. Some brands of doenjang can be very strong (especially artisanal ones that have been made using traditional processes), but any brand available at a Korean or Asian grocery stores should be on the milder end of the spectrum.

Ganjang

While broadly considered 'soy sauce', Korean ganjang has its own distinct character. Traditionally, it's the liquid byproduct that's extracted during doenjang production, which results in a sauce that is deeper, more complex and often saltier than commercial soy sauces. There are different types, including guk ganjang which is generally used for cooking heartier dishes like soups and braises, and jin ganjang, which is slightly milder so is better for more general cooking and dipping sauces. Ganjang is used in virtually every Korean dish, from marinades for Bulgogi (grilled marinated beef, page 124) to seasoning stir-fries, soups, dipping sauces and vegetable side dishes.

These three ingredients are not just flavour enhancers; they are living foods, packed with beneficial probiotics thanks to the fermentation process.

BAECHU KIMCHI

SEOUL-STYLE KIMCHI

For Koreans, kimchi is deeply personal and incredibly significant. It's often said that Koreans can't truly enjoy a meal without it. Far more than just food, this iconic fermented cabbage staple is a way of life! It's on every table, at every meal – a constant companion that reflects the seasons and family traditions. Kimchi embodies resilience (fermented to last through harsh winters), community (the annual Kimjang kimchi-making event brings families and neighbours together), and identity for many Koreans.

While countless kimchi variations exist across Korea, Seoul-style baechu kimchi stands out. It's known for its refreshing crunch and perfect balance of spicy, savoury and tangy flavours, often featuring a vibrant red colour and a slightly less overwhelmingly salty profile compared to some other regional kimchi variations.

Tasting baechu kimchi is to taste the very essence of Korea – a living, breathing cultural symbol that continues to evolve, yet remains utterly indispensable.

MAKES 5 KG (11 LB)

- 500 g (1 lb 2 oz) coarse sea salt, plus extra for sprinkling
- 5 kg (11 lb) wombok (Chinese cabbage), about 2–3 heads

Salting the cabbage

1 Place the coarse sea salt in a large food-grade bag or Korean kimjang bag. (Traditionally, people used large earthenware fermentation pots known as onggi, or big round rubber buckets.) Add 2 litres (2 quarts) water and stir until the salt dissolves to create a brine.

2 Rinse the cabbages to remove any surface dirt. Cut the cabbage heads in half lengthways; if they're very large, you can quarter them. Sprinkle extra handfuls of coarse sea salt between the thicker stem parts.

3 Submerge the cabbage pieces into the brine in the bag. Seal the bag and roll the cabbage within the bag to ensure the brine evenly saturates all parts.

4 Arrange the cabbage so that the sturdy core parts are facing downwards. Leave to salt in a cool dark spot for 8–12 hours, or until the leaves are flexible and can bend easily without breaking. (Leaving the cabbage in a warm spot could cause premature fermentation, which is why kimchi is traditionally made during winter.) During this time, flip the cabbage occasionally, without opening the bag, for even salting – simply roll the bag over to evenly distribute the brine.

Rice paste

360 ml (12 fl oz) water

3 tablespoons glutinous rice flour

Kimchi seasoning

225 g (8 oz) gochugaru (Korean chilli flakes)

50 g (1¾ oz) minced garlic

15 g (½ oz) minced ginger

1 tablespoon coarse sea salt

75 g (2¾ oz) saeujeot (salted fermented shrimp)

150 ml (5 fl oz) anchovy fish sauce (myeolchi aekjeot)

100 g (3½ oz) tuna extract (chamchi-aek)

50 ml (1¾ fl oz) maesil cheong (green plum extract)

½ Korean pear (or ½ sweet apple), grated

5 Rinse the salted cabbage three or four times under cold running water to wash off the excess salt and any impurities. After rinsing, it's essential to drain the cabbage thoroughly, to prevent spoilage. Place the cabbage upside down on a drying rack or a colander to allow all water to completely drip out. Excess water can dilute the kimchi paste and promote the growth of unwanted bacteria.

Make the kimchi seasoning

1 Place the rice paste ingredients in a small saucepan and whisk until smooth. Cook over medium-low heat, stirring constantly, until the mixture thickens into a smooth paste. Turn off the heat and leave to cool completely.

2 Measure 180 ml (6 fl oz) of the cooled rice paste into a large bowl. Add 200 g (7 oz) of the gochugaru and mix well. Allow the mixture to sit for at least 30 minutes to 1 hour, to allow the chilli to fully hydrate and deepen in colour.

3 Add the rest of the kimchi seasoning ingredients, including the remaining gochugaru, and mix thoroughly.

Continues next page →

Kimchi filling

- ½ Korean radish, cut into long, thin strips
- 1 bunch (15–20) jjokpa (slender spring onions/scallions), cut into 3 cm (1¼ in) lengths
- 1 white onion, thinly sliced
- 240 ml (8 fl oz) Anchovy-kelp broth (page 192)
- 360 ml (12 fl oz) water

Prepare the kimchi filling

1 Stir all the kimchi filling ingredients into the seasoning mixture.

2 Before stuffing the cabbage, taste a small piece of the seasoned filling mixture. It should taste a bit stronger and saltier than you think is necessary, as the salt will be absorbed by the cabbage over time. It should be savoury, spicy and slightly sweet, but with a noticeable salty punch. If it seems too bland, add a little more anchovy fish sauce or coarse sea salt; a pinch of sugar can also be added for balance.

Prepare and store the kimchi

1 Sterilise a 5–6 litre (5–6 quart) food-grade container (or several smaller ones) with boiling water.

2 Lightly spread the kimchi filling on the inner, yellowish leaves of the drained cabbage pieces. Work your way outwards, generously spreading the seasoning evenly between each leaf.

3 Once the cabbage pieces are stuffed, gently fold the outer, greener leaves over the seasoned inner leaves to tuck them in.

4 Place the cabbage in your sterilised container, packing it in tightly to squeeze out any air pockets. Use some of the outer leaves from the salted cabbage to cover the kimchi. This prevents the kimchi being directly exposed to air, helping it store better.

5 Seal the container/s tightly to prevent air entering and to contain all the fermenting aromas. Leave to ferment at room temperature out of direct sunlight for 1–2 days, briefly opening the lid every now and then to release the built-up gas, so the container doesn't become too pressurised.

6 After 1–2 days at room temperature, transfer the container/s to the fridge, where the kimchi will keep for several months. The flavour will continue to develop and become more sour over time; you can use this 'fermented kimchi' for cooking dishes such as Dwaejigogi kimchi jjigae (pork kimchi stew, page 81) and Spam kimchi bokkeumbap (Spam kimchi fried rice, page 64).

7 Once the container is opened, the kimchi will still keep for months if you always use a clean utensil to remove the kimchi and reseal the container tightly each time.

NABAK KIMCHI

WATER KIMCHI

Nabak kimchi is a popular variety of mul-kimchi, or water kimchi, that originated in Seoul. Unlike many other types of kimchi, it's not spicy, and is enjoyed instead for its mild, refreshing flavour and abundant, watery broth.

The term 'nabak' comes from the Korean verb nabak-nabak, meaning to thinly and squarely slice something – referring to the cabbage and radish in this kimchi.

One of the great things about nabak kimchi is that it's very quick to ferment – it only needs a day or two – and can be enjoyed any time of the year. Whereas many other kimchi varieties contain fermented fish sauce (jeotgal), nabak kimchi is typically made without it, relying on salt, sugar and chilli powder (or fresh red chilli) to flavour the refreshing liquid. This results in a crisp, clean taste, making this kimchi perfect as a palate cleanser.

SERVES 10 AS A SIDE DISH

- 1 head of wombok (Chinese cabbage), about 450 g (1 lb)
- 300 g (10½ oz) Korean radish, peeled and cut into 2–3 cm (¾–1¼ in) squares, about 2 mm (1⁄12 in) thick
- 3 tablespoons coarse sea salt
- 10 jjokpa (slender spring onions/scallions), cut into 3 cm (1¼ in) lengths
- ½ carrot, cut into 2–3 cm (¾–1¼ in) squares, about 2 mm (1⁄12 in) thick
- 3 green chillies, thinly sliced; for a cleaner broth, remove the seeds
- 2 tablespoons maesil cheong (green plum extract)
- 1 tablespoon coarse sea salt

Kimchi seasoning

- ½ Korean pear (or ½ sweet apple)
- ½ onion, roughly chopped
- 7 garlic cloves, peeled
- 2 red chillies, stems removed
- 20 g (¾ oz) piece fresh ginger, peeled
- 1 tablespoon cooked rice

1 Sterilise a 5 litre (5 quart) food-grade container (or several smaller ones) with boiling water.

2 Cut the core out of the cabbage so the leaves separate naturally, then slice the leaves into bite-sized squares.

3 Place the cabbage and radish in the sterilised container. Sprinkle 1 tablespoon of the coarse sea salt over the radish and the remaining salt over the cabbage. Leave to sit, uncovered, for 30 minutes, then mix together the cabbage and radish to ensure they are evenly salted.

4 To make the kimchi seasoning, place the pear and onion in a blender with the garlic, chillies, ginger and rice. Blend until completely smooth, then pour the mixture through a fine-mesh sieve directly over the salted cabbage and radish. Gently press on the pulp in the sieve to extract all the liquid and flavour. Discard the remaining pulp.

5 Pour 4 litres (4 quarts) water into the container. Add the jjokpa, carrot and green chilli.

6 Stir in the maesil cheong and salt. Adjust the salt and maesil cheong to achieve a taste that is pleasantly sweet and salty before the kimchi starts to ferment; the goal for nabak kimchi is a balance of refreshing sweetness, mild spiciness and a clean, tangy sourness from the fermentation.

7 Seal the container, transfer to the fridge and leave to ferment for 1–2 days to allow the flavours to deepen before serving, after which time the nabak kimchi will be at its most refreshing and delicious. Since the fermentation process is quick and light, opening the lid once or twice during the first day will be enough to release the gas. The bubbles you see forming on the surface are a completely natural and desired result of fermentation – a positive sign your kimchi is 'ripening', developing its characteristic sour and tangy flavour and reaching its peak nutritional benefit.

8 Once opened, the nabak kimchi will maintain its cool, crisp, refreshing flavour for 2–3 weeks in the fridge if you take care to always use a clean utensil to remove the kimchi, and reseal the container tightly each time.

KKAKDUGI

DICED RADISH KIMCHI

This isn't your typical leafy kimchi: it's a bold, vibrant and satisfyingly crunchy radish kimchi that delivers a refreshing kick! Kkakdugi rose to fame as the perfect companion to hearty Korean stews and rich, milky soups such as Seolleongtang (ox bone soup, page 88), where its crisp, tangy, refreshing bite cuts through the richness and keeps your palate perfectly balanced. It's no surprise it became a must-have at Seoul's famous seolleongtang restaurants (before it spread to dining tables across the country), with one common saying declaring that a seolleongtang restaurant can only truly succeed if its kkakdugi is delicious.

Today, it's one of the most common types of kimchi you'll find – a flavourful reminder that sometimes the simplest pairings are the most powerful and delicious!

MAKES 4 KG (8 LB 13 OZ)

- 4 kg (8 lb 13 oz) white Korean radish
- 80 g (2¾ oz) coarse sea salt
- 40 g (1½ oz) white sugar
- 100 g (3½ oz) jjokpa (slender spring onions/scallions), or 3–5 regular spring onions

Seasoning mix

- 2 tablespoons cooked rice (see Note)
- ½ large Korean pear (or ½ large sweet apple), about 200 g (7 oz)
- ½ white onion, roughly chopped
- 4 tablespoons saeujeot (salted fermented shrimp)
- 100 g (1 cup) coarse gochugaru (Korean chilli flakes)
- 80 ml (⅓ cup) maesil cheong (green plum extract)
- 4 tablespoons minced garlic
- 1 tablespoon minced ginger
- 80 ml (⅓ cup) anchovy fish sauce (myeolchi aekjeot)

Note
Don't omit the cooked rice in the seasoning mix. The starch from the rice helps the seasoning bind and aids fermentation.

1 Wash the radish thoroughly, leaving the skin on for extra flavour and crunch. Cut the radish into 2.5 cm (1 in) cubes.

2 Place the radish in a large bowl with the coarse sea salt and sugar. Mix well to ensure the radish is evenly coated. Leave to sit for 2 hours, tossing once or twice to ensure even brining.

3 Transfer the radish to a colander to drain. There's no need to rinse it.

4 Wash the spring onions and cut into 3 cm (1¼ in) lengths. Set aside.

5 To make the seasoning mix, place the cooked rice in a blender with the pear, onion and saeujeot. Blend until smooth, then transfer to a large bowl. Add the remaining ingredients and mix thoroughly to create a paste.

6 Add the drained radish to the seasoning paste. Mix thoroughly, ensuring every piece of radish is evenly coated. Gently mix the spring onion through.

7 Taste the mixture. If it seems bland, add a pinch more coarse sea salt at a time, mixing well, until the desired level of saltiness is reached.

8 Transfer to a 5 litre (5 quart) airtight food-grade container that has been sterilised with boiling water. Pack the kkakdugi tightly into the container, pressing down firmly to remove any air pockets. This helps the flavours meld and improves the kimchi's storage life. Seal the container/s tightly to prevent air entering and to contain all the fermenting aromas.

9 Leave to ferment at room temperature out of direct sunlight for 1–2 days, briefly opening the lid every now and then to release the built-up gas, so the container doesn't become too pressurised. You'll know it's ready to go into the fridge when it starts to smell slightly sour and you see small bubbles rising in the liquid. Taste a piece; it should have a pleasant tangy flavour.

10 Transfer to the fridge, where the kkakdugi will keep for several months, fermenting slowly and developing deeper and more sour flavours over time – a desirable characteristic of fermented kimchi.

OI MUCHIM
CUCUMBER SALAD

A delightful side that brightens any meal, this popular salad is a staple in Korean homes, cherished for its hydrating crunch and vibrant, tangy and subtly spicy dressing. Incredibly versatile and easy to make, it's the perfect palate cleanser and a wonderful way to awaken your appetite, especially on hot summer days or when you need a light, refreshing counterpoint to richer dishes.

SERVES 4 AS A SIDE DISH

3 short cucumbers
1½ tablespoons coarse sea salt
1 onion, thinly sliced lengthways
1 large spring onion (scallion), white part only, very thinly sliced
sesame oil, for drizzling
toasted sesame seeds, for sprinkling

Seasoning

2½ tablespoons gochugaru (Korean chilli flakes)
1½ tablespoons gochujang (Korean chilli paste)
1½ tablespoons maesil cheong (green plum extract)
1½ tablespoons rice vinegar
1½ tablespoons minced garlic
1½ tablespoons white sugar
1½ teaspoons jin ganjang (Korean soy sauce)
1½ teaspoons anchovy fish sauce (myeolchi aekjeot)

1 Wash the cucumbers and dry them thoroughly. Slice into 1 cm (½ in) thick rounds and place in a bowl. Add the sea salt and gently toss to coat, then leave to sit for about 10 minutes to draw out the excess moisture.

2 Lightly rinse the cucumber slices under cold running water to remove the excess salt. Transfer to a colander and leave to drain thoroughly, to remove as much water as possible.

3 While the cucumbers are draining, mix all the seasoning ingredients together in a bowl. Leave to sit for about 10 minutes, to let the gochugaru soften and the flavours meld.

4 Transfer the drained cucumber to a large mixing bowl. Add the onion and spring onion. Pour the seasoning mixture over the vegetables. Using clean hands (wearing gloves is recommended), toss and mix together thoroughly until all the vegetables are evenly coated with the seasoning.

5 Drizzle with a touch of sesame oil and sprinkle with toasted sesame seeds. Enjoy immediately as a refreshing side dish.

YACHAE JANGAJJI

PICKLED VEGETABLES

Unlike more complex fermented foods, these quick and easy pickles, often featuring crisp cucumbers, sweet onions and mild green chillies, are typically made by simply steeping fresh vegetables in a savoury, tangy and slightly sweet soy sauce-based brine. The result? A burst of clean, refreshing flavour and a satisfying crunch that makes any meal more exciting.

This simple yet incredibly versatile banchan (side dish) is a staple in Korean homes, perfect for those moments when you need something light, refreshing, or just a little something extra to kickstart your appetite.

MAKES A 1.5 LITRE (6 CUP) JAR

- 2 white onions, peeled
- 2 short cucumbers
- 6 mild green chillies
- 220 g (1 cup) white sugar
- 250 ml (1 cup) jin ganjang (Korean soy sauce)
- 250 ml (1 cup) rice vinegar
- 125 ml (½ cup) maesil cheong (green plum extract)

1 Thoroughly wash the onions, cucumbers and chillies. Pat them dry with paper towel or a clean cloth, ensuring the vegetables are completely dry, for longer preservation.

2 Cut the onions in half and remove the cores, then cut each onion half into eight wedges, then into 2 cm (¾ in) chunks. Slice the cucumbers and chillies into 1 cm (½ in) thick pieces.

3 In a saucepan, combine the sugar, soy sauce and 500 ml (2 cups) water over medium heat, stirring until the sugar dissolves.

4 Turn off the heat, then stir in the vinegar and maesil cheong. (Adding the vinegar once the heat is turned off helps to preserve its acidity, resulting in a more vibrant sour pickle flavour.)

5 Arrange the cut vegetables neatly into a 1.5 litre (6 cup) sterilised glass jar or airtight container. Pour the hot brine over the vegetables. It's fine if they are not initially completely submerged – as the vegetables pickle, they will release moisture and eventually become fully submerged. Leave to cool completely to room temperature.

6 Once cooled, seal the jar or container and refrigerate for at least 1 day before serving. The salt, sugar and vinegar in the brine act as preservatives, so the pickles will keep in the fridge for up to 3 months or even longer if stored properly. The vegetables will soften over time, but the pickle will continue to develop a deeper flavour. For best results, always use a clean utensil when taking the pickles out, and keep the vegetables fully submerged in the brine.

GIM GUI

TOASTED SEAWEED

A versatile staple enjoyed throughout the day, these lightly oiled and salted toasted seaweed sheets are generally enjoyed as a simple side dish (banchan) or savoury snack, and are often crumbled or cut into fine strips as a flavourful garnish for dishes such as tteokguk (sliced rice cake soup, page 36).

Gim gui also holds a special place in Korean hearts as a simple yet profound gesture of love, often handmade by mothers or grandmothers for their children or grandchildren.

MAKES ABOUT 48 PIECES

- 60 ml (¼ cup) perilla oil
- 60 ml (¼ cup) sesame oil
- 8 sheets saeng-gim (raw seaweed sheets, see Note)
- ½ teaspoon fine sea salt

1 In a small bowl, combine the perilla oil and sesame oil. Set aside.

2 Place one sheet of seaweed on a flat tray or clean surface. Using a pastry brush, carefully and evenly spread a thin layer of the oil mixture over the seaweed sheet, then evenly sprinkle a pinch of salt over the oiled surface.

3 Place another sheet of seaweed directly on top of it. Repeat the oiling and salting process, layering all eight sheets on top of one another, ensuring each sheet is oiled and salted on one side before the next sheet is placed on top.

4 Let the stacked seaweed sheets rest for at least 15 minutes. This allows the salt to dissolve and the oil to evenly soak into the seaweed, preventing it tasting overly salty and ensuring even toasting.

5 Heat a frying pan large enough to fit a whole seaweed sheet over medium heat.

6 Once the pan is hot, reduce the heat to low. Place one seaweed sheet, oiled side down, onto the hot pan. Using a spatula, gently press down on the seaweed to ensure even contact with the pan. Toast until the seaweed turns a vibrant green colour – this indicates it's properly toasted. Flip and quickly toast the other side until it also turns vibrant green, but be careful not to over-toast, as the seaweed can quickly burn and become bitter. Keep the heat low and watch carefully.

7 Quickly remove from the pan, to a cutting board, and toast the remaining seaweed sheets in the same way.

8 Let the toasted seaweed cool to room temperature, before using a knife to cut each sheet into six rectangular pieces. Allowing the sheets to cool properly makes them much firmer and more brittle, so you can easily cut them into neat squares or strips.

9 Store in an airtight container or zip-lock bag in a cool, dry place. When properly stored, your gim gui should maintain its crispiness for 2–3 weeks. The key is to prevent any moisture getting in, as this will make the seaweed soften and lose its crunch. For best results, store with silica gel packets.

Note

In Korean, these 'raw' seaweed sheets are known as saeng-gim. Unseasoned, untoasted seaweed sheets are widely available from Asian grocery stores.

GYERAN-JANG

SOY-MARINATED EGGS

Gyeran-jang is a popular yet incredibly simple Korean side dish. Soft-boiled eggs are marinated in a savoury, slightly sweet soy sauce mixture. The tender yolks and rich, flavourful marinade make these eggs an irresistible accompaniment to a bowl of warm rice.

MAKES 8

- 8 × 60 g (2 oz) eggs, at room temperature
- 1 teaspoon salt
- 1 teaspoon vinegar

Marinade

- 100 ml (3½ fl oz) jin ganjang (Korean soy sauce)
- 100 ml (3½ fl oz) water
- 50 ml (1¾ fl oz) mirim (Korean cooking rice wine)
- 2 tablespoons white sugar
- ½ onion, finely chopped
- 2 spring onions (scallions), finely chopped
- 1 green chilli, finely chopped
- 2 garlic cloves, minced
- 1 teaspoon toasted sesame seeds

1 Place the eggs in a saucepan and cover with enough cold water to fully submerge them. Add the salt (this helps the shells peel off easily) and vinegar (to help the egg whites set and stop them leaking if the shells crack).

2 Bring the water to a boil, then leave to boil for 5–6 minutes for a soft-boiled yolk. Immediately transfer the eggs to an ice bath to stop the cooking process. Once cooled, carefully peel the eggs.

3 Place the marinade ingredients in a container large enough to hold all the eggs. Thoroughly mix the marinade ingredients together until the sugar has dissolved.

4 Gently place the peeled eggs into the marinade, making sure they are well submerged. Do not use any eggs that are cracked or broken, as the yolks will leak out and make the marinade cloudy and it will cause the dish to spoil more quickly. Seal the container and transfer to the fridge.

5 After 2–3 hours, gently turn the eggs to ensure they are evenly marinated. For the best flavour, let them marinate for at least half a day before serving. The eggs will keep in an airtight container in the fridge for up to 3–4 days.

6 When ready to serve, slice the eggs in half to reveal the rich, jammy yolks.

MYEOLCHI BOKKEUM

STIR-FRIED SMALL DRIED ANCHOVIES

This simple stir-fried anchovy dish holds a surprisingly big place in Korean hearts! These tiny, crispy morsels aren't just a side dish; they're a nostalgic bite of childhood for many Koreans, as this dish was often lovingly prepared by mothers to ensure their kids got their calcium. Myeolchi bokkeum embodies the warmth of Korean home cooking, showing how even the smallest, humblest dish can carry immense cultural charm.

SERVES 4 AS A SIDE DISH

200 g (7 oz) small dried anchovies
2 tablespoons vegetable oil
1 tablespoon jin ganjang (Korean soy sauce)
1 tablespoon white sugar
⅓ large spring onion (scallion), white part only, thinly sliced
¼ teaspoon minced garlic
1 tablespoon oligo syrup
sesame oil, for drizzling
toasted sesame seeds, for sprinkling
chopped mixed nuts, such as walnuts or almonds, to serve (optional)

1 Place the anchovies in a sieve set over a tray. Lightly shake the sieve to release any leftover fish particles or powder.

2 Heat a frying pan over medium-low heat without any oil. Dry-roast the anchovies for about 3 minutes, stirring occasionally, until they are crispy and any fishy odour is reduced; this step is essential for removing the fishy smell.

3 Place the toasted anchovies in the sieve one more time to shake off any remaining fine powder.

4 Clean out the frying pan and place over medium heat. Add the toasted anchovies and the vegetable oil and stir gently to coat the anchovies in the oil.

5 Push the anchovies to one side of the pan, then pour the jin ganjang directly onto the exposed hot surface of the pan. Let it bubble intensely for a few seconds to create a deeper, richer 'fire taste', then quickly stir it into the anchovies and add the sugar.

6 Add the spring onion and garlic, stirring well. Finally, add the oligo syrup and a drizzle of sesame oil and continue to stir-fry briefly until the anchovies are glossy and well-coated.

7 Transfer to a serving dish and sprinkle generously with toasted sesame seeds. If desired, you can also sprinkle with chopped nuts for extra crunch and flavour.

BAPSIM

THE POWER OF RICE

For thousands of years, rice has been the staple grain of the Korean diet. This crop is deeply entwined with the country's agricultural history and daily life. Rice serves as the foundation upon which almost every Korean meal is built.

In Korean culture, the word 'bap' means much more than just 'rice'. It commonly refers to an entire meal itself, encompassing not just the grain but a sense of nourishment, comfort and the act of eating together. This profound connection is best captured by the concept of bapsim – literally, 'the power of rice'.

Bapsim recognises that rice is not merely a carbohydrate; it is the fundamental source of daily energy, strength and overall well-being for Koreans. It embodies the belief that a good, hearty bowl of rice provides the sustenance needed to power through the day, overcome challenges and maintain good health. When someone feels weak or tired, a common saying is, 'you need your bapsim!', meaning you need to eat a good meal, centred around rice, to regain your strength.

Bap is way more than just food here – it's the secret handshake of Korean culture! Koreans often ask 'Bap meogeosseoyo?' (Have you eaten rice?) instead of 'How are you?' as a greeting. And it's not just a way of asking about how hungry you are, it's a genuine way to check in and see if you are doing okay. Are you healthy? If you've eaten, it's assumed all's well. If not? Expect immediate concern and maybe even an offer to share a meal! It's our unique way of showing we care.

When Koreans want to connect with friends, they'll say 'Bap hanbeon meokja' (Let's eat bap sometime). It's a warm, casual invitation to connect, share stories and build a stronger bond. The unspoken meaning is something like: 'I value our relationship, and I want to spend quality time with you over a meal.' It's all about communal dining, good conversation and fostering those connections.

So next time you share a meal in Korea, remember: you're not just eating. You're participating in a rich cultural exchange where rice is the silent, yet powerful, medium for care, connection, and the very essence of life itself. Enjoy your bap!

영산암보살
010-3691-2341
卍 영산암
卍 영산암
010-3691-2341
卍
영
산
암
卍 영산암

BAP

RICE

For Koreans, 'bap' is more than just rice – it's the heart of life. Bap is at the very core of Korean cuisine, right alongside kimchi. No matter how many delicious side dishes there are, a meal isn't complete without bap. Every soup, stew and side dish is made to be eaten with rice. Bap isn't just an ingredient; it's the very soul and foundation of Korean food culture. For a nation with a long history of food shortages, eating rice was crucial for staying alive and healthy. That's why asking 'Did you eat bap?' isn't just a casual greeting; it's a warm way of showing you care about someone's health and happiness. Even a simple 'Let's eat bap sometime' is more than an invitation to eat; it's an offer to connect and build a friendship. Eating bap with family, friends or colleagues is a powerful way to strengthen bonds. Most importantly, the warm bap prepared by a mother or grandmother is a silent, powerful message of unconditional love. A love letter you can taste.

SERVES 4

440 g (2 cups) short-grain white rice

500 ml (2 cups) cold water, approximately, plus more for rinsing

1 Place the rice in a bowl. Cover with cold water and gently swirl the rice with your hand to clean the rice without breaking the grains. Drain the rice then repeat the rinsing process three or four times until the water runs mostly clear.

2 Transfer the rinsed rice to a colander. Let the rice drain and 'dry soak' for 30 minutes. (This 'dry soaking' allows the grains to swell slightly and absorb water more evenly during cooking, resulting in a superior texture.)

3 Transfer the rice to a saucepan with a tight-fitting lid. Add the measured cold water (maintaining a 1:1 ratio with the original dry rice volume); the water should cover the rice by about 1.5 cm (½ in).

4 Place the pan on the stove over high heat with the lid off. Bring the water to a rolling boil, watching carefully, as it can boil over quickly.

5 Once the water reaches a strong boil with large, active bubbles, reduce the heat to medium. Place the lid on tightly and cook for 10 minutes. Do not lift the lid during this step!

6 After 10 minutes on medium heat, reduce the heat to the lowest possible setting for a very gentle simmer. Keep the lid on tightly and continue to cook for another 10 minutes.

7 After this time, turn off the heat completely, but keep the lid on. Let the rice rest and steam for 10–15 minutes. This final resting period is crucial, allowing the steam to fully penetrate and fluff up the grains evenly.

8 Remove the lid. Using a rice paddle or spatula, gently fluff the rice from the bottom up. This releases excess steam and prevents the rice clumping.

9 Serve immediately, with your favourite Korean dishes!

JAPGOKBAP

MULTIGRAIN RICE

In Korean homes, when a mother serves this dish instead of plain white rice, it's a quiet but powerful act of love and care. This isn't just about adding flavour; it's a mindful choice for the family's health, helping them build good eating habits from the very beginning.

Unlike simple white rice, japgokbap is a nutritious blend of various grains such as brown rice, black beans, millet and barley. This makes it naturally richer in essential nutrients such as fibre, vitamins and minerals. It's a fantastic choice for supporting overall health, aiding digestion, and particularly, helping to manage blood sugar levels. For family members concerned with conditions like diabetes, japgokbap becomes an important, thoughtful part of their diet.

So, when you see a bowl of japgokbap, know it's more than just a meal; it's a mother's way of nurturing her family's well-being, proving that even a simple bowl of rice can be packed with love, care and nutrition.

SERVES 4

330 g (1½ cups) short-grain white rice

150 g (¾ cup) mixed dried grains, such as black rice, brown rice, barley, black beans (use your favourite blend!)

840 ml (28½ fl oz) cold water, approximately (see method)

1 Combine the white rice and mixed grains in a large bowl. Rinse thoroughly under cold running water, gently swirling the grains with your hand. Since whole grains often have husks or tougher outer layers compared to white rice, it's good to wash them more carefully.

2 Discard the cloudy water. Repeat this process five or six times until the water runs mostly clear.

3 Transfer the rinsed grains to a saucepan with a tight-fitting lid. Add the cold water, bearing in mind that different grains absorb water differently. If your mixture is mostly white rice and quick-cooking grains, a ratio of 1:1.2 (1.2 times as much water as rice and grains) is ideal – so 675 ml (23 fl oz) water might be enough. If your mixture has a lot of tougher grains such as brown rice or black beans, a ratio closer to 1:1.5 (1.5 times as much water as rice and grains) works best, so use closer to 840 ml (28½ fl oz) water. A traditional way to check the water ratio is with your finger. After adding the soaked grains and water to your pan, gently rest the tip of your index finger on the surface of the rice. The water level should reach the first joint of your finger. For Koreans, this is a reliable visual guide for cooking rice on the stovetop.

4 Let the grains soak for at least 30 minutes. (In warmer weather, 20 minutes might be enough, but in colder winter months, they'll need 30 minutes or more.)

5 Place the pan on the stove over high heat, with the lid off. Bring the water to a rolling boil, watching carefully, as it can boil over quickly.

6 Once the water reaches a strong boil with large, active bubbles, reduce the heat to medium and place the lid on tightly. Do not lift the lid during this step! Let it simmer gently for 10 minutes.

7 After 10 minutes on medium heat, reduce the heat to the lowest possible setting for a very gentle simmer. Keep the lid on tightly and continue to cook for another 10 minutes.

8 After this time, turn off the heat completely, but keep the lid on. Let the rice and grains rest and steam for 10–15 minutes. This final resting period is crucial, allowing the remaining steam to fully penetrate and fluff up all the grains evenly.

9 Remove the lid. Using a rice paddle or spatula, gently fluff the rice and grains from the bottom up to release excess steam and ensure an even, perfectly cooked texture.

10 Serve immediately with your favourite Korean dishes!

BUCHIMGARU

KOREAN PANCAKE MIX

Achieve perfectly crispy and delicious Korean pancakes with this specially formulated pancake mix. This convenient mix ensures the ideal texture and flavour for a wide variety of 'jeon' (pancakes), from savoury vegetable pancakes to crispy seafood renditions. It's the key to quick and satisfying Korean comfort food.

MAKES 250 G (9 OZ)

- 200 g (1⅓ cups) plain (all-purpose) flour
- 30 g (1 oz) glutinous rice flour
- 2 tablespoons potato starch
- 2 teaspoons onion powder
- 1 teaspoon salt
- 1 teaspoon garlic powder
- ½ teaspoon white sugar
- ¼ teaspoon finely ground black pepper

1 Combine all the ingredients in a large bowl.

2 Use a whisk to thoroughly combine all the ingredients. Make sure there are no lumps and the salt is evenly distributed.

3 Transfer the mixture to an airtight container. It will keep in a cool, dry place for 3–6 months, just like store-bought flour.

창

MYEOLCHI-DASIMA YUKSU

ANCHOVY- KELP BROTH

Unlock the secret to countless Korean dishes with this essential magic broth. Made from dried anchovies and kelp, this versatile stock forms the deeply umami and savoury base for almost every Korean soup and stew.

MAKES 1.5 LITRES (6 CUPS)

- 200 g (7 oz) dashi anchovies (large dried anchovies for broth)
- 2 large spring onion (scallion) roots
- 1 white onion, unpeeled
- 30 g (1 oz) dasima (dried kelp)
- 2 large pieces of Korean radish, about 3 cm (1¼ in) thick
- 2 litres (2 quarts) cold water

1 Remove the anchovy heads by pinching them off. Gently press on the belly to split the anchovies in half and carefully remove the dark inner intestines. (The intestines can cause bitterness.)

2 Heat a dry, ungreased frying pan over medium heat. Add the cleaned anchovies and lightly pan-fry them for a few minutes until they become fragrant. This step helps to evaporate any residual moisture and also reduce any potential fishy smell.

3 Thoroughly clean the spring onion roots with a brush to remove any soil. Thoroughly wash the onion (with its skin on) and cut it in half.

4 Lightly moisten a paper towel and gently wipe the surface of the dasima to remove any impurities - but do not rinse under water, as this washes away the white powdery film, which is rich in umami.

5 In a large deep saucepan, combine the pan-fried anchovies, spring onion roots, onion halves, dried kelp and radish. Pour in the water.

6 Place the pan over high heat and bring to the boil. After 10 minutes, remove the dasima. (Leaving kelp in for too long can result in a slimy broth and a slightly bitter taste.)

7 Reduce the heat to medium-low and let the broth simmer gently for 20 minutes. Do not simmer for too long at this point, as this can also lead to a bitter taste from the anchovies.

8 Turn off the heat and allow the broth to cool slightly. Line a fine-mesh sieve with clean muslin (cheesecloth) and set over a large bowl, then carefully strain the broth through the sieve, discarding all the solids.

9 Once completely cooled, transfer the clear anchovy broth to an airtight container. It will keep in the fridge for up to 1 week.

YAK-GOCHUJANG

SEASONED CHILLI PASTE

Elevate your simple rice bowl with this flavourful twist on traditional gochujang. This 'medicinal' or 'nutritious' chilli paste often incorporates minced beef and other seasonings, transforming plain rice into a satisfying meal. It's a go-to secret kick in the Korean kitchen, perfect when you need a quick, delicious meal with few other side dishes.

MAKES ABOUT 400 G (14 OZ)

- vegetable oil, for cooking
- 50 g (1¾ oz) chopped spring onions (scallions)
- 1 tablespoon minced garlic
- 200 g (7 oz) minced (ground) beef
- 150 g (5½ oz) gochujang (Korean chilli paste)
- 2 tablespoons jin ganjang (Korean soy sauce)
- 3 tablespoons mirim (Korean cooking rice wine)
- 1 tablespoon maesil cheong (green plum extract)
- 1 tablespoon oligo syrup
- sesame oil, for drizzling
- toasted sesame seeds, for sprinkling

1 Heat a little vegetable oil in a frying pan over medium heat. Saute the chopped spring onion and garlic for 3–5 minutes, to infuse the oil with their aroma.

2 Add the beef and cook for 5–10 minutes, stirring now and then, until evenly browned.

3 Reduce the heat to low, add the gochujang, jin ganjang, mirim, maesil cheong and oligo syrup. Stir well and simmer for another 5–10 minutes, until thickened.

4 Turn off the heat, then finish with a drizzle of sesame oil and a sprinkling of sesame seeds.

5 Leave to cool completely, then transfer to an airtight container. The paste will keep in the fridge for up to 2 weeks.

CHOGOCHU-JANG

RED PEPPER PASTE MIXED WITH VINEGAR

Korea's vibrant and versatile dipping sauce, chogochujang is a zesty, tangy and slightly sweet blend of gochujang and vinegar. Perfect for fresh hoe (raw fish sashimi), seafood and crisp raw vegetables, its unique balance of spicy, sour and savoury flavours will awaken your palate. This indispensable sauce is a must-try for exploring the dynamic tastes of Korean cuisine!

MAKES ABOUT 130 G (4½ OZ)

3 tablespoons gochujang (Korean chilli paste)

2 tablespoons rice vinegar

1 tablespoon maesil cheong (green plum extract)

1 tablespoon fizzy lemon-lime-flavoured soft drink, such as Sprite

1 teaspoon sesame oil

1 teaspoon white sugar

1 teaspoon toasted sesame seeds

1 teaspoon minced garlic

1 Combine all the ingredients in a bowl.

2 Mix well until all the ingredients are thoroughly combined and the sugar is fully dissolved.

3 Transfer to an airtight container. The paste will keep in the fridge for up to 2 weeks.

SSAMJANG

SEASONED BEAN PASTE

No Korean barbecue experience is complete without this rich, savoury and subtly spicy dipping sauce. This essential condiment, typically a blend of doenjang and gochujang, garlic and sesame oil, is crucial for building the perfect ssam (lettuce wrap). It's the unifying flavour that brings all the elements together.

MAKES ABOUT 200 G (7 OZ)

125 g (½ cup) doenjang (Korean soybean paste)

2 tablespoons gochujang (Korean chilli paste)

1 tablespoon minced garlic

1 tablespoon finely chopped spring onion (scallion)

1 tablespoon sesame oil

1 tablespoon toasted sesame seeds

1 teaspoon oligo syrup

1 In a small bowl, combine the doenjang and gochujang.

2 Add the remaining ingredients and mix thoroughly until well combined.

3 If the ssamjang is too thick, mix in 1–2 tablespoons water.

4 Transfer to a small serving bowl and serve as a dipping sauce.

CHOGANJANG

VINEGARED SOY SAUCE

Typically a mix of soy sauce, vinegar and often chilli flakes, this simple yet essential soy sauce-based condiment provides a clean, tangy and savoury counterpoint to many Korean dishes. It's the versatile dipping partner for everything from crispy pancakes to steamed dumplings.

MAKES ABOUT 80 ML (2½ FL OZ)

- 3 tablespoons jin ganjang (Korean soy sauce)
- 2 tablespoons rice vinegar
- 1 teaspoon maesil cheong (green plum extract)
- 1 teaspoon toasted sesame seeds
- pinch of gochugaru (Korean chilli flakes)

1 In a small bowl, combine the soy sauce, vinegar and maesil cheong.

2 Stir in the sesame seeds and a pinch of gochugaru and mix together gently.

3 Serve immediately as a dipping sauce.

YANGNYEOM GANJANG

SEASONED SOY SAUCE

This isn't regular soy sauce; it's an incredibly versatile, vibrant, ready-to-use blend designed to instantly elevate dishes. A secret weapon in countless homes, use it as a dipping sauce for dumplings, and for seasoning noodle dishes, vegetable side dishes such as Samsaek namul (page 40) and tofu- or potato-based braises.

MAKES ABOUT 200 ML (7 FL OZ)

- 2 tablespoons finely chopped spring onion (scallion), white part only
- 1 tablespoon minced garlic
- 80 ml (⅓ cup) jin ganjang (Korean soy sauce)
- 1 tablespoon water
- 1 tablespoon sesame oil
- 1 tablespoon gochugaru (Korean chilli flakes)
- 1 tablespoon toasted sesame seeds
- 1 teaspoon rice vinegar
- ½ teaspoon white sugar

1 Place the spring onion, garlic, jin ganjang, water, sesame oil, gochugaru and sesame seeds in a small bowl. Stir until well combined. Add the vinegar and sugar and mix again.

2 Let the sauce sit for 5–10 minutes before serving to allow the flavours to meld.

3 The sauce will keep in the fridge in an airtight container for up to 1 week.

MATGANJANG

FLAVOURFUL SOY SAUCE

Discover the secret weapon of many Korean home cooks: matganjang. This 'flavourful soy sauce' is often infused with umami-rich ingredients such as kelp, anchovies or vegetables, making it a versatile shortcut for enhancing the depth of countless dishes, simplifying cooking while boosting flavour.

Add a tablespoon or two to soups, stews and stir-fried dishes. Matganjang can also be used in braised dishes and as a base for meat marinades.

MAKES 800 ML (27 FL OZ)

- 1 onion, peeled and halved
- 1 large spring onion (scallion), cut into large pieces
- 6 garlic cloves, peeled and lightly smashed
- 20 g (¾ oz) fresh ginger, peeled and thinly sliced
- 3 dried shiitake mushrooms
- 1 piece dasima (dried kelp), about 5 cm (2 in) square
- 500 ml (2 cups) jin ganjang (Korean soy sauce)
- 125 ml (½ cup) mirim (Korean cooking rice wine)
- 60 ml (¼ cup) cheongju (Korean rice wine)
- 55 g (¼ cup) white sugar

1 Place all the ingredients in a large saucepan. Add 250 ml (1 cup) water and bring to the boil over medium-high heat.

2 Once the liquid starts boiling, reduce the heat to medium-low and let it simmer gently for 10 minutes.

3 After 10 minutes, remove the dasima. (Leaving kelp in for too long can result in a slimy sauce with a slightly bitter taste.)

4 Leave to simmer for a further 10–15 minutes, to allow all the flavours to meld and infuse into the soy sauce base. Do not boil on high heat, as this can reduce the volume of the sauce too much and make it overly salty.

5 Turn off the heat and let the sauce cool slightly. Carefully strain through a fine-mesh sieve into a clean heatproof jar, discarding all the solids. This will leave you with a clear, flavourful liquid.

6 Allow to cool completely to room temperature before storing in the fridge. It will keep for up to 2 weeks in a clean sealed jar.

MATGANJAN

GLOSSARY

The following are common ingredients in Korean cooking that can be found in Asian and Korean grocery stores or greengrocers.

Banchan

A collective term for the small, accompanying side dishes served with a Korean meal. They provide variety and balance to the main course.

Bap

Rice – no meal in Korea is complete without it!

Buchu

Also known as Korean chives, these flat, long tender stems have a strong, pungent flavour that is a cross between onion and garlic.

Chamchi-aek

A seasoning sauce that is similar to fish sauce, but made from fermented tuna and salt. It adds a deep umami flavour.

Cheongju

A clear Korean rice wine, often used in cooking to tenderise meat and remove gamey odours. It's also enjoyed as a beverage.

Dangmyeon

Korean glass noodles made from sweet potato starch. They have a chewy, texture and become translucent when cooked and are famously used in Japchae.

Dasima

A type of dried kelp with a deep umami flavour. It is often used to make a savoury broths (yuksu) for soups and stews.

Doenjang

Korean fermented soybean paste, a fundamental ingredient in Korean cooking known for its deep, earthy flavour, which is similar to Japanese miso.

Eomuk

These processed seafood cakes are made from pureed fish or other seafood that has been mixed with a starchy ingredient. They have a slightly elastic texture and are often used in soups and various street foods.

Gim

Dried seaweed, commonly used in various Korean dishes, most notably for wrapping gimbap. It has a slightly savoury, oceanic flavour.

Gochugaru

Korean chilli flakes or chilli powder, a staple ingredient that provides the signature spicy and vibrant red colour to many Korean dishes like kimchi and stews.

Gochujang

Korean chilli paste, a savoury, sweet and spicy fermented condiment made from chilli powder, glutinous rice, fermented soybeans and salt.

Gosari

Fern bracken, a common wild edible plant in Korea, often prepared as a seasoned side dish (namul) after being rehydrated and cooked.

Guk ganjang

Korean soup soy sauce, a lighter, saltier soy sauce primarily used for seasoning soups and stews without darkening the broth too much. It has a distinct flavour.

Jin ganjang

Korean regular soy sauce, a versatile all-purpose soy sauce widely used in Korean cooking for seasoning, marinades and sauces. It provides a foundational savoury flavour to many Korean dishes.

Jjokpa

Small spring onion (scallion), a slender green onion variety used extensively in Korean cuisine for flavour, garnish and texture.

Kimchi

This iconic fermented wombok (Chinese cabbage) dish is far more than just a side dish; it's a way of life in Korea, embodying resilience, community and identity. Kimchi is on every table at every meal. There are many variations of kimchi, some recipes include different vegetables.

Maesil cheong

Korean green plum extract, a sweet and tangy syrup made from green plums, used as a natural sweetener and flavour enhancer in various Korean dishes and beverages.

Makgeolli

Korean rice wine, a milky, lightly carbonated and subtly sweet alcoholic beverage made from fermented rice. It's a traditional drink often paired with savoury pancakes.

Miyeok

Dried seaweed, specifically brown seaweed, which is full of minerals and nutrients. Miyeok is used to make soups like Sogogi miyeok guk (beef seaweed soup).

Mirim

Korean cooking rice wine. Mirim is a type of sweet rice wine similar to Japanese mirin, used in cooking to tenderise meat, remove odours and add a subtle sweetness and glaze.

Myeolchi aekjeot

A type of fish sauce made from fermented anchovies.

Oligo syrup

Short for oligosaccharide syrup, oligo syrup is a less sweet and healthier alternative to corn syrup. It is often used in Korean cooking to give dishes a subtle sweetness. It is also very helpful at giving sauces a glossy finish.

Perilla leaves

A fragrant, serrated leaf with a unique, pungent aroma. Perilla leaves are commonly used in Korean cuisine as a wrap for grilled meats (called a 'ssam') or as a herb in various dishes.

Perilla seed oil

Perilla seed oil, a distinctively nutty and aromatic oil pressed from perilla seeds, often used as a finishing oil to add flavour to Korean dishes.

Saeujeot

A fermented condiment made from tiny salted shrimp, used to add a savoury, umami flavour and depth to kimchi and various Korean dishes.

Sagol gomtang yuksu

Beef bone broth, specifically made from ox leg bones, simmered for a long time to produce a rich, milky and nourishing broth, often used as a base for soups.

Soju

A clear, distilled alcoholic beverage, often called Korea's national drink. It is commonly paired with various Korean dishes, especially spicy stews.

Ssam

This word means 'wrapped' and refers to the delightful act of wrapping your grilled meat (or other fillings) in crisp lettuce or perilla leaves. It's a core interactive part of Korean BBQ.

Wombok (Chinese cabbage)

Wombok is a cabbage with broad, pale green leaves. Also called Napa cabbage in some parts of the world, this is the main ingredient in one of Seoul's most iconic dishes, Baechu kimchi.

Yeondu

A fermented bean essence, often used as a vegetarian or vegan alternative to fish sauce or other umami enhancers in Korean cooking. It provides a savoury depth.

Yeot-gireum

Malted barley powder, a key ingredient for making Sikhye (sweet rice punch). It helps in the enzymatic process that converts rice starch into sugars.

ABOUT THE AUTHOR

Julian Kim is the founder of Seoul Cooking Club, a top-rated culinary experience in Korea dedicated to helping international visitors understand Korean culture through the rituals, stories and philosophy that surrounds Korean food. Though not a classically trained chef, he is widely recognised in Seoul as a culinary storyteller, food entrepreneur and cultural ambassador.

Julian spent more than sixteen years abroad in cities such as London, Abu Dhabi, Shanghai and Almaty, where he immersed himself in diverse food cultures and developed a deep appreciation for how cuisine reflects identity.

After returning to Korea, Julian began hosting food tours that introduced visitors to Seoul's markets, traditional eateries and regional specialties. His storytelling-based approach quickly gained wide acclaim, eventually inspiring the creation of Seoul Cooking Club: an immersive cooking studio where guests learn authentic Korean dishes hands-on while discovering the cultural wisdom behind them.

Julian later founded Seoul Dining Group to expand Korean culinary culture overseas through thoughtful restaurant concepts and collaborations. His recent projects include Bapzip (a modern interpretation of traditional Korean dining) and Seoul Bundt (a Korean reimagining of the classic bundt cake), as well as culinary consulting for global restaurateurs seeking authentic Korean flavours and techniques.

Julian's mission is to make sure that Korean food is not only enjoyed, but understood – to show that Korea's food culture is a living expression of the country's spirit, which is meant to be experienced, remembered and passed on.

ACKNOWLEDGEMENTS

Julian would like to express his gratitude to the team at Seoul Cooking Club, whose passion for hospitality and teaching played a central role in the development of this book.

INDEX

T

V

W

Y

Z

Published in 2026 by Smith Street Books
Naarm (Melbourne) | Australia
smithstreetbooks.com

Distributed outside of ANZ, North & Latin America by
Thames & Hudson Ltd., 6–24 Britannia Street, London, WC1X 9JD
thamesandhudson.com

EU Authorised Representative: Interart S.A.R.L.
19 rue Charles Auray, 93500 Pantin, Paris, France
productsafety@thameshudson.co.uk; www.interart.fr

ISBN: 978-1-9232-3986-9

Smith Street Books respectfully acknowledges the Wurundjeri People of the Kulin Nation, who are the Traditional Owners of the land on which we work, and we pay our respects to their Elders past and present.

Publisher: Megan Cuthbert
Project editor: Elena Callcott
Editor: Katri Hilden
Design and layout: Murray Batten
Food photography: Rochelle Eagle
Stylist: Lee Blaylock
Recipe development: Elly Shin, Olivia Kim, Grace Sim and Sally Yun
Food preparation: Caroline Griffiths and Melanie Ryan
Indexer: Max McMaster
Proofreader: Pamela Dunne
Production manager: Aisling Coughlan
Pre-press: Megan Ellis

Printed & bound in China by C&C Offset Printing Co., Ltd.

Book 446
10 9 8 7 6 5 4 3 2 1

MIX
Paper | Supporting responsible forestry
FSC® C008047